Colors of the Garden:

Lessons in Art

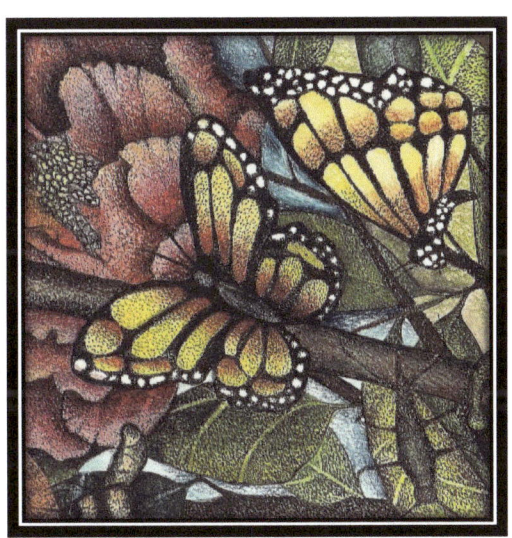

by

Jan Brieschke

Colors of the Garden: Lessons in Art

ISBN: 9798325948497

Jan Brieschke – janbrieschkeartist@gmail.com

Dedication

There are those who come into our lives, and although they stay just a short time, they leave memories that last a lifetime.

This is true of my dog, Jackie, who I had from a small puppy until her death at eleven years old. She was my constant companion and best friend. I'll never forget her.

A sweet and loving creature, she was also my protector. She was always vigilant, but always ready to play.

She loved the outdoors and she loved our walks in the garden.

This book is dedicated to Jackie (named after the artist Jackson Pollack). She will always be at my side.

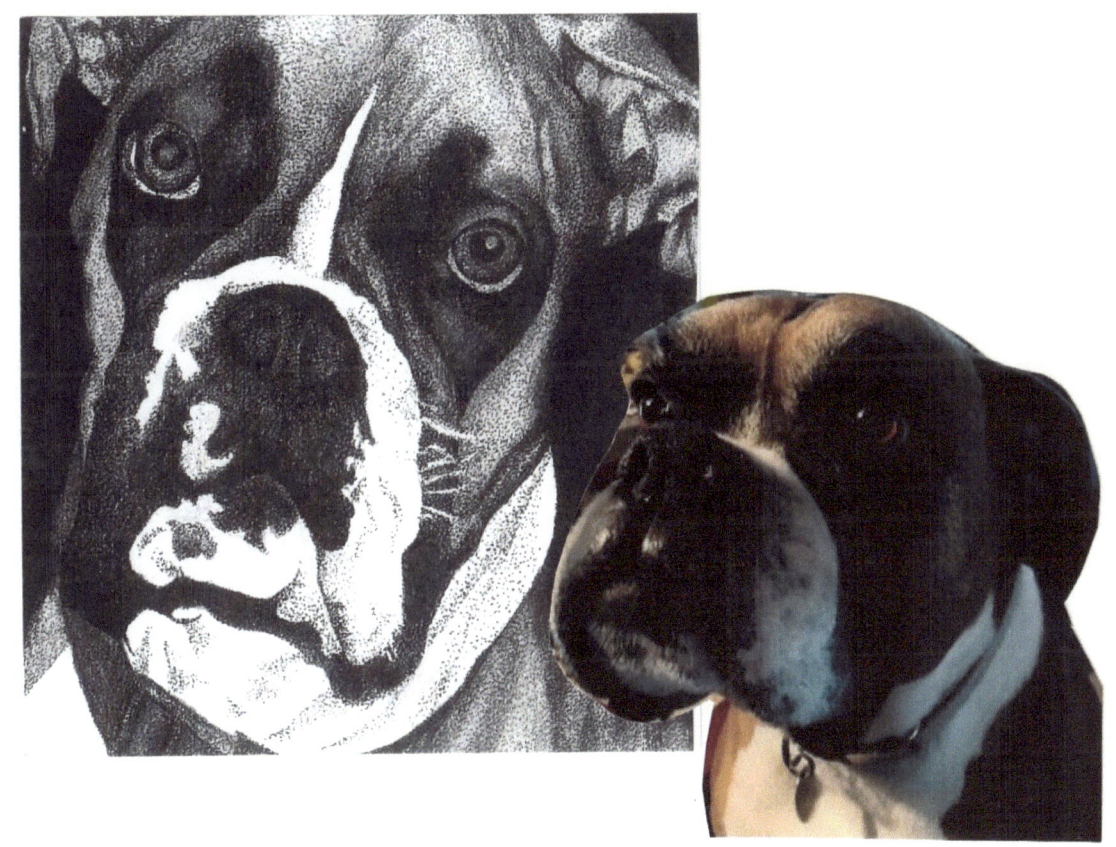

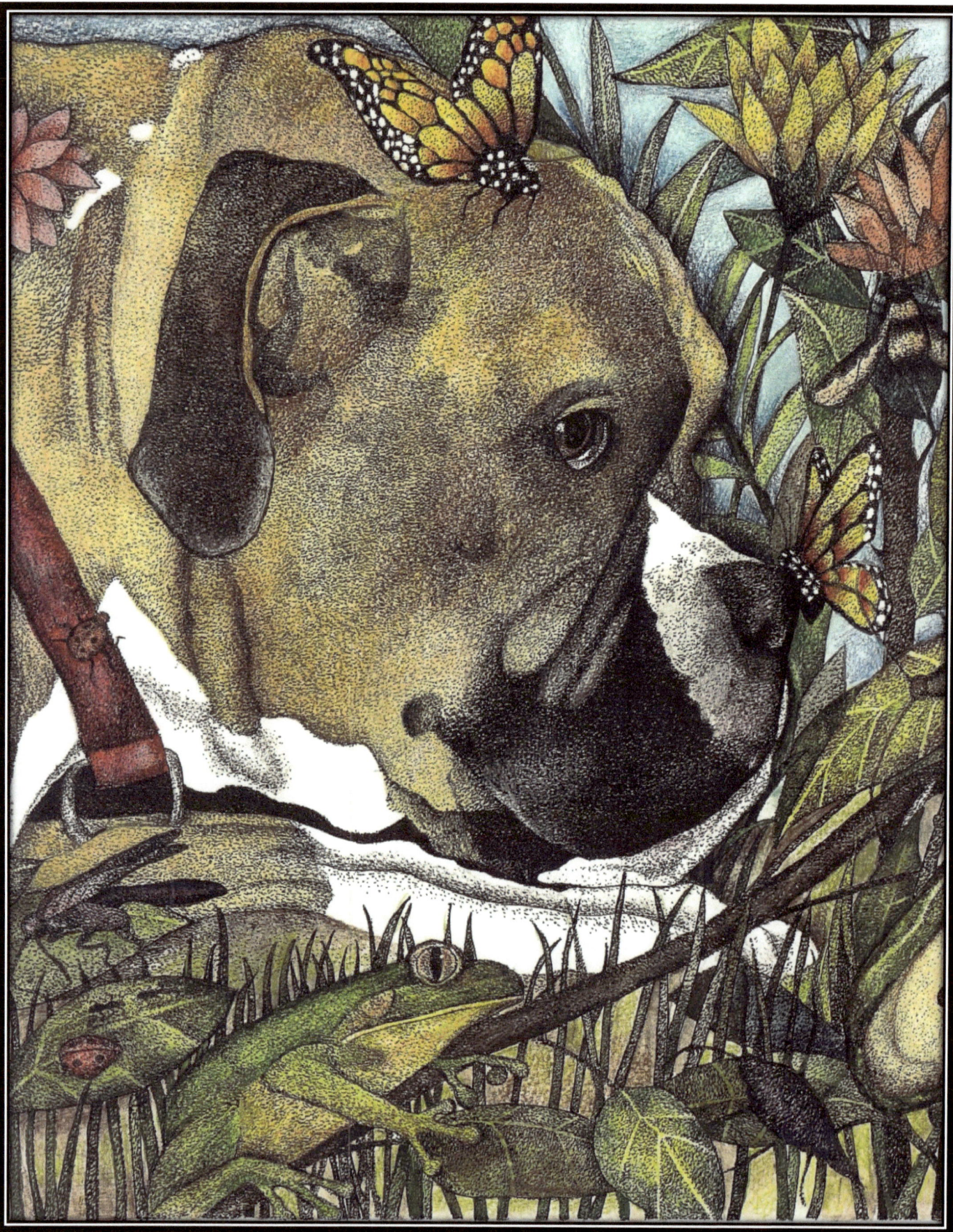

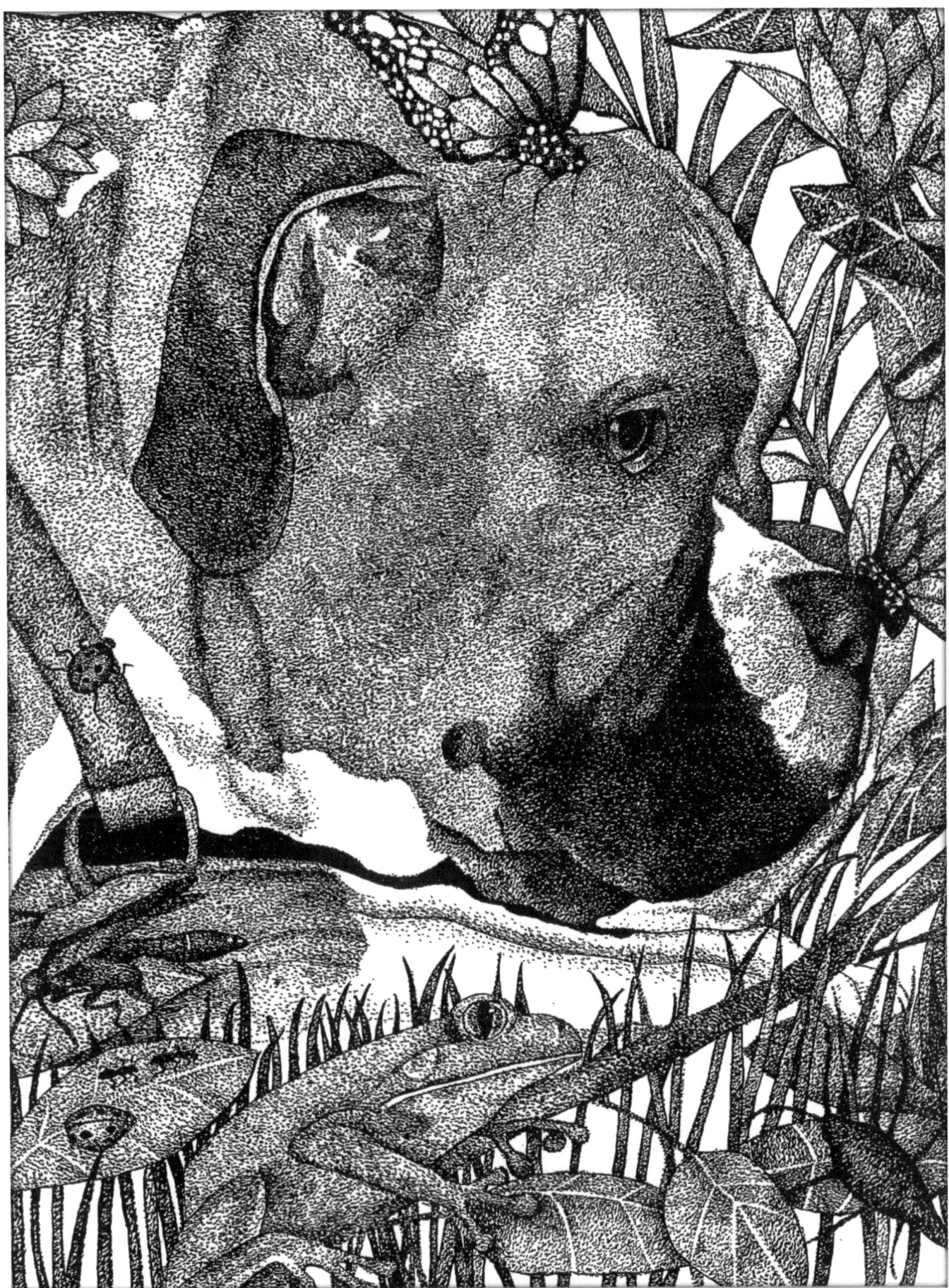

Building a Garden

To create this book, I used a variety of tools. I used Micron pens in sizes .005 and .01 on the initial drawings in the stippling technique. Stipplings are entirely made of tiny dots. When an artist wants to create dark areas, he uses more dots and the dots are closer together. To create lighter areas, he uses few dots.

I included colored examples of each drawing, so that you could see how they could look with colored pencil shading over the pen and ink. By no means do I mean for you to color the drawings exactly as I have done. Use your own imagination. I prefer colored pencils when doing this technique for the detail and intensity that can be achieved.

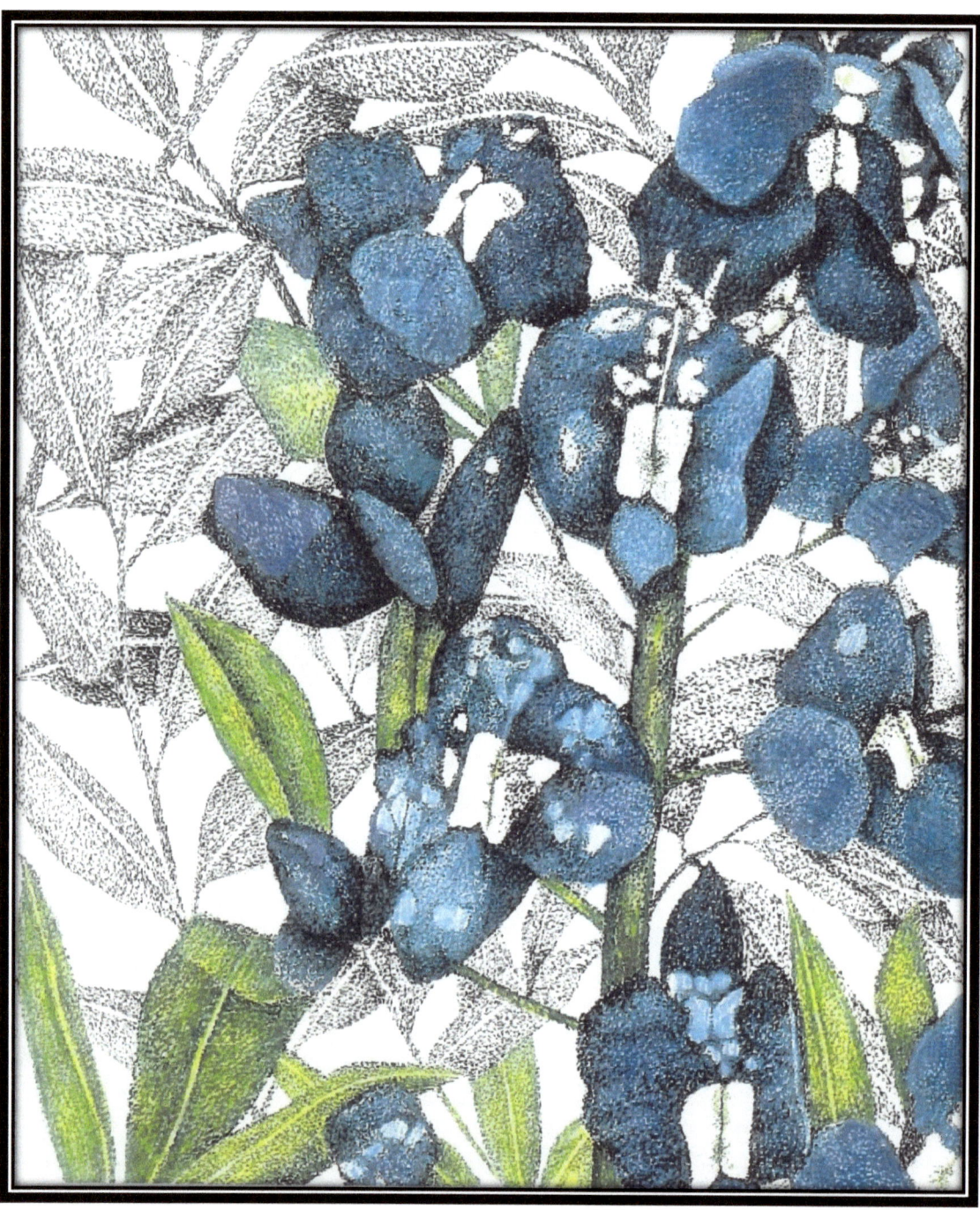

Color Wheel

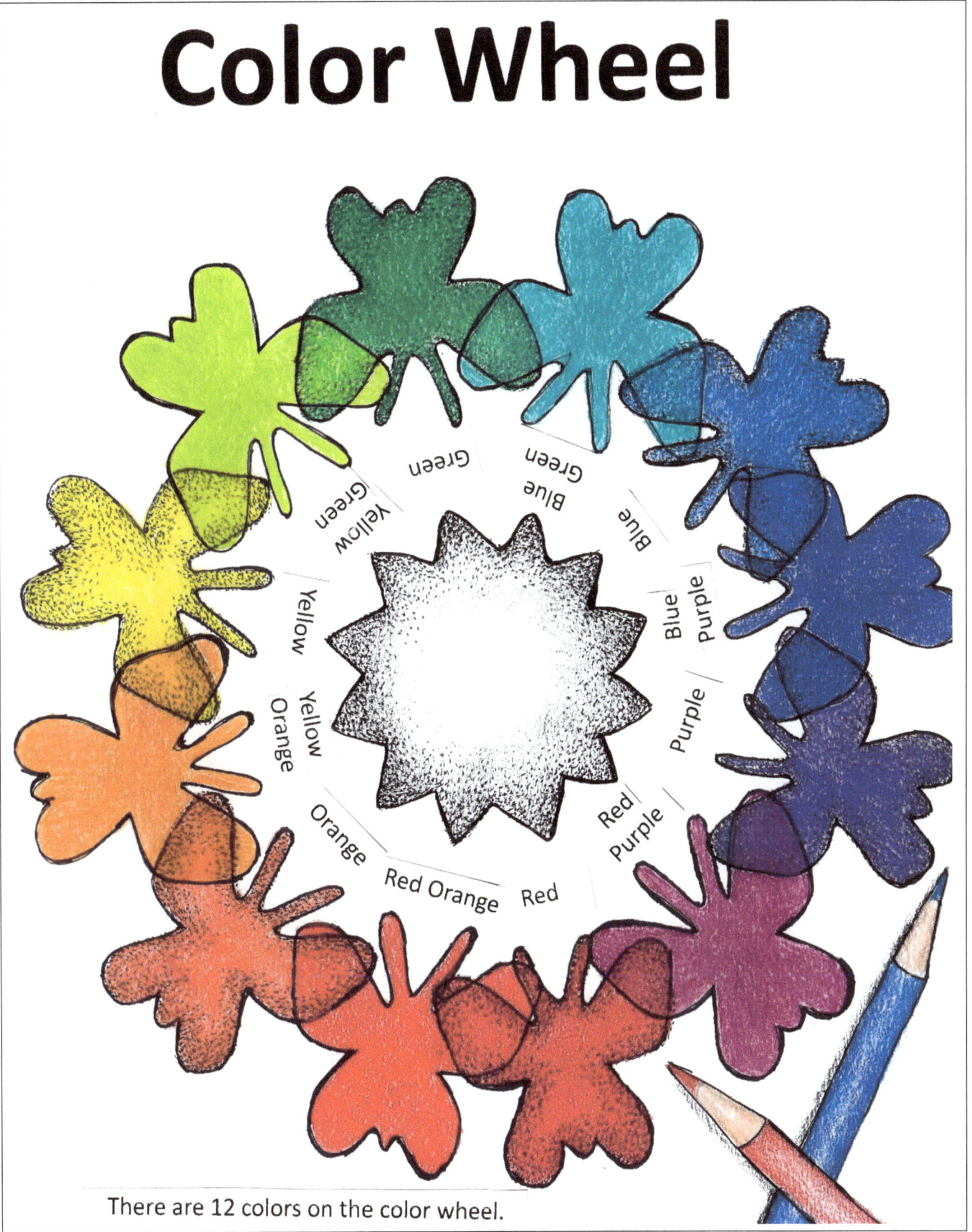

The labels on the wheel read (clockwise from top): Yellow Green, Green, Blue Green, Blue, Blue Purple, Purple, Red Purple, Red, Red Orange, Orange, Yellow Orange, Yellow

There are 12 colors on the color wheel.

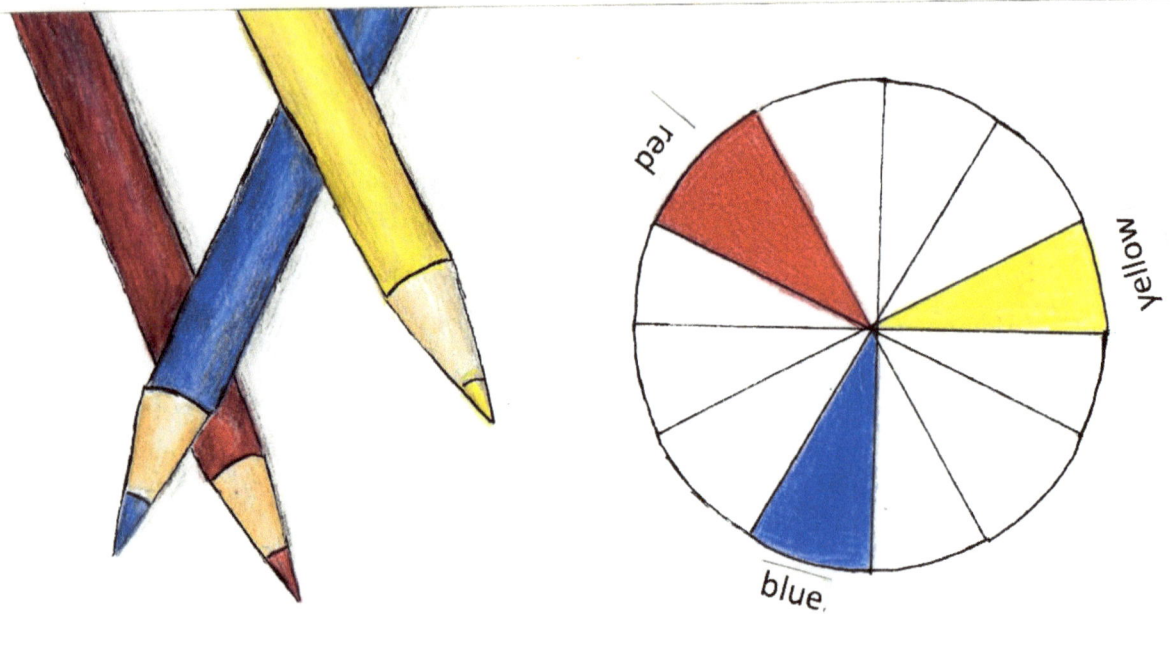

The three primary colors (used to make all the other colors).

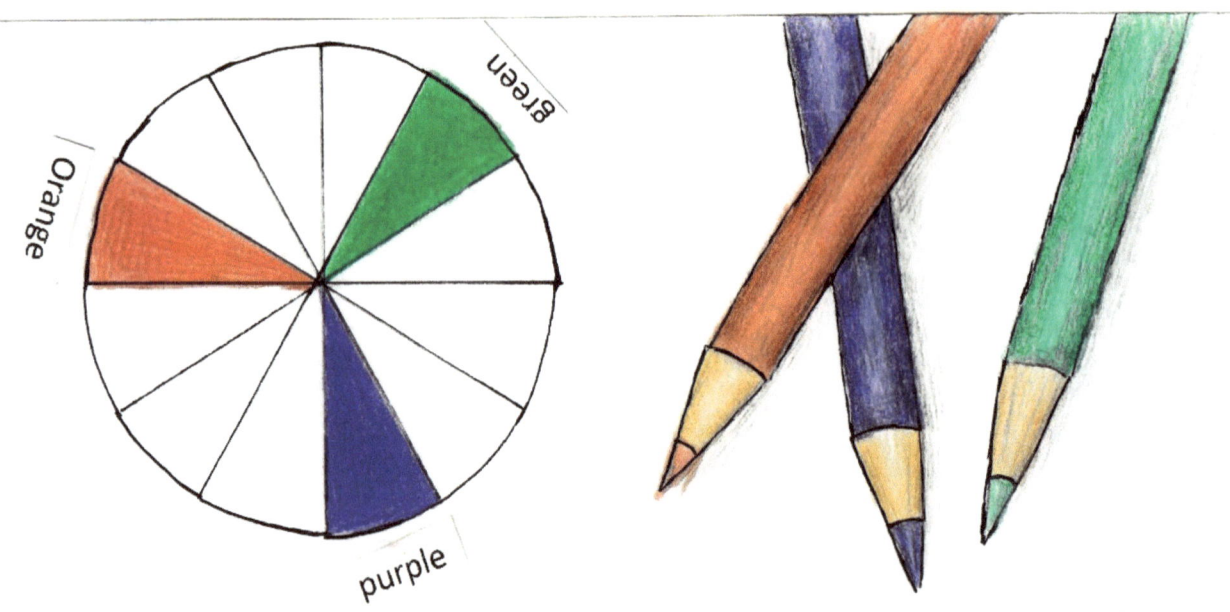

There are three secondary colors (formed by mixing two of the primary colors).

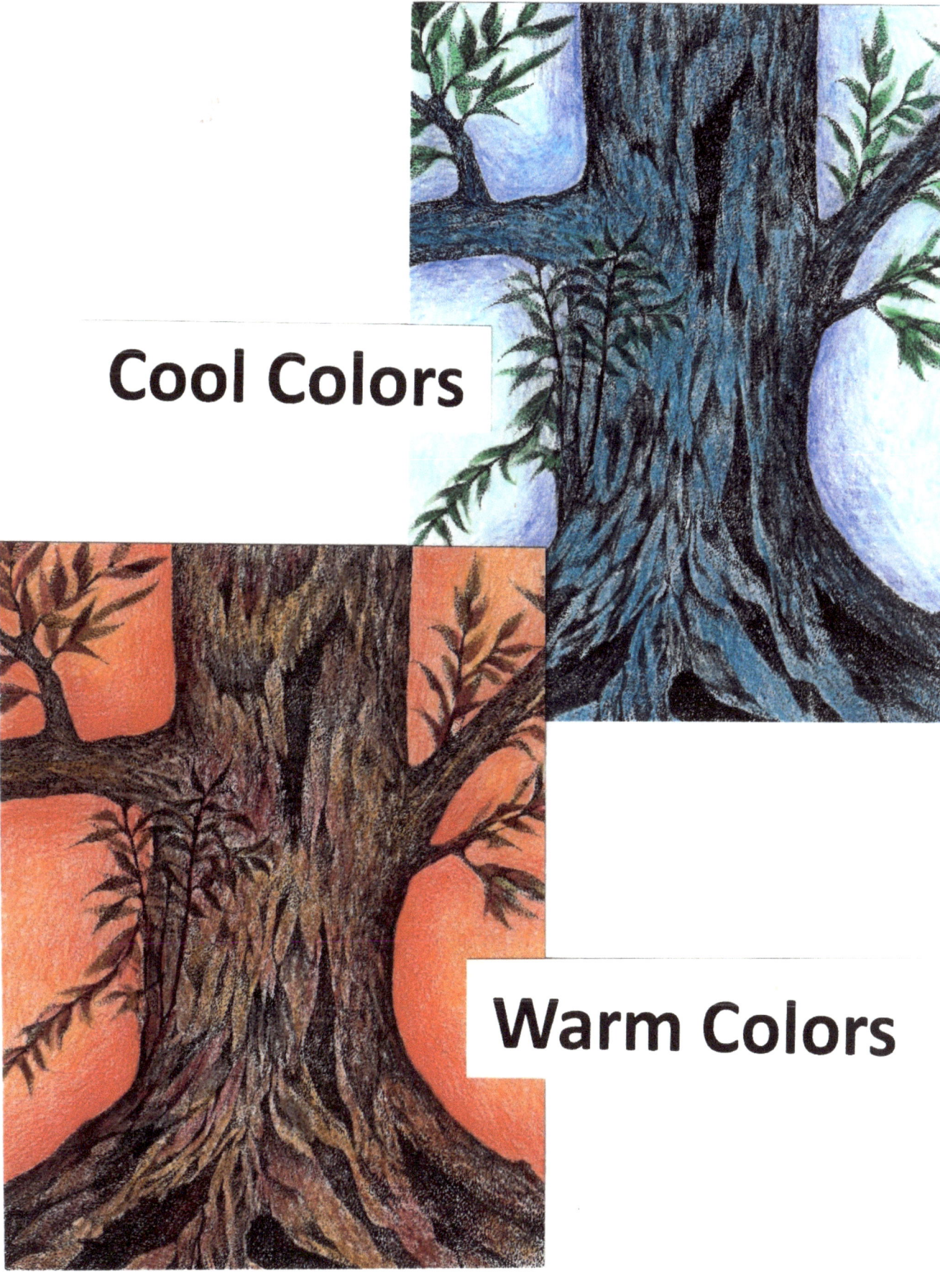

Cool Colors

Warm Colors

Color Schemes

Monochromatic

A monochromatic color scheme is formed by the use of one color plus black and white.

I used yellow, black, and white.

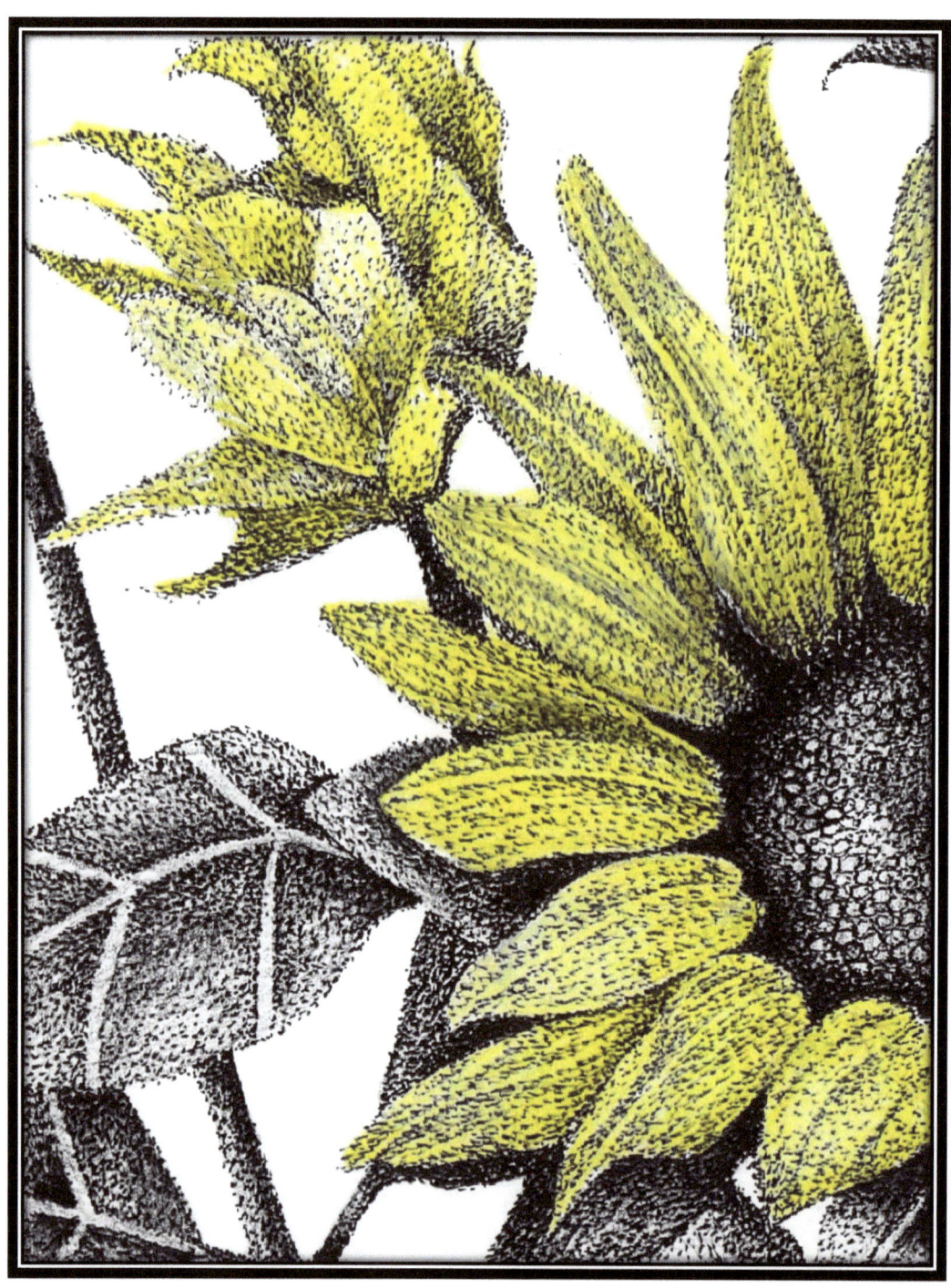

Analogous

An analogous color scheme is created by using two or three colors that are next to each other on the color wheel. Again, black and white can be used.

I used yellow, yellow orange, and orange, along with black and white.

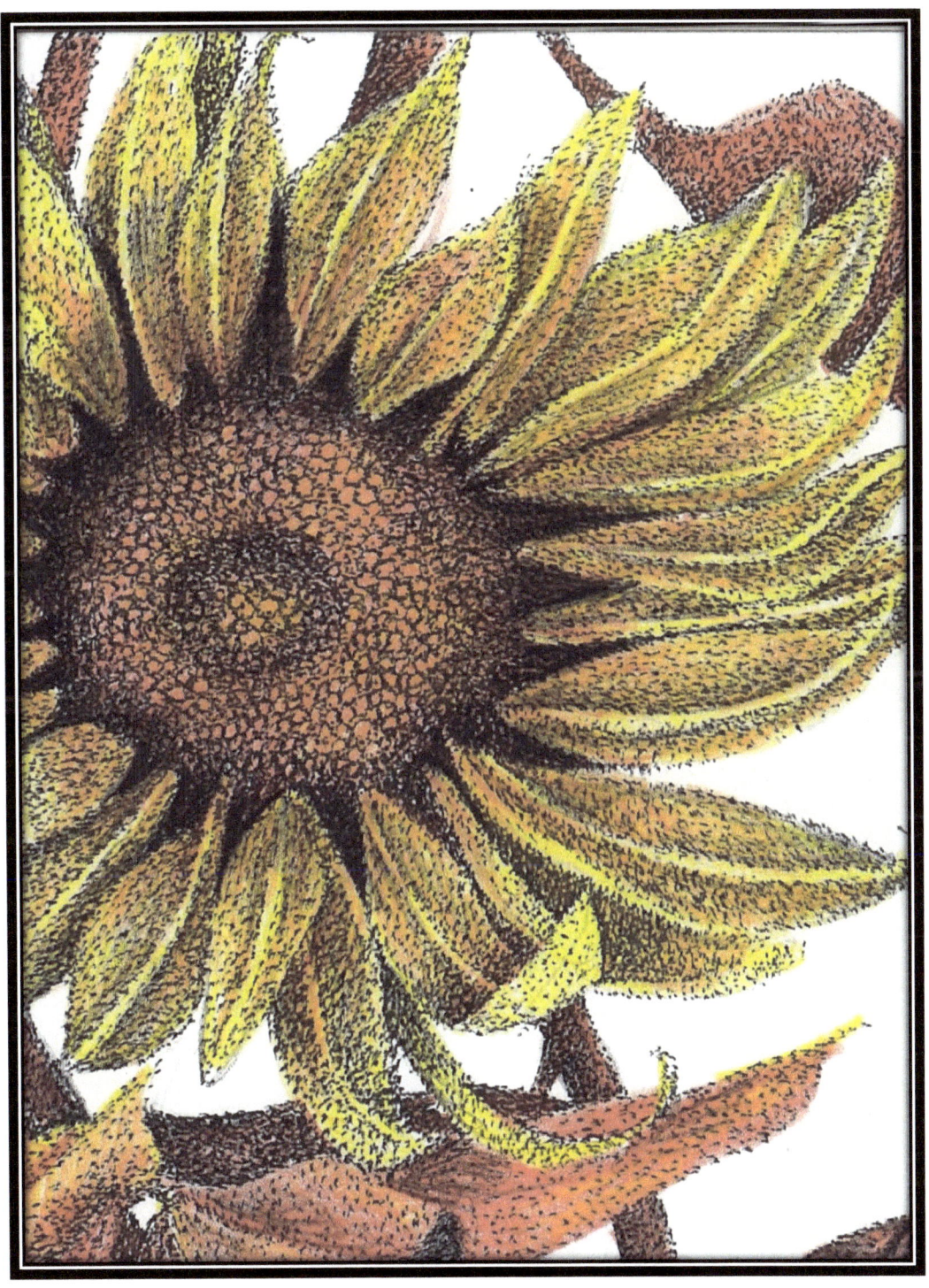

Complementary

A complementary color scheme consists of two colors that are directly opposite each other on the color wheel. Black and white can also be used to make the colors lighter or darker or to create purely black or white areas.

I used purple and yellow, black and white.

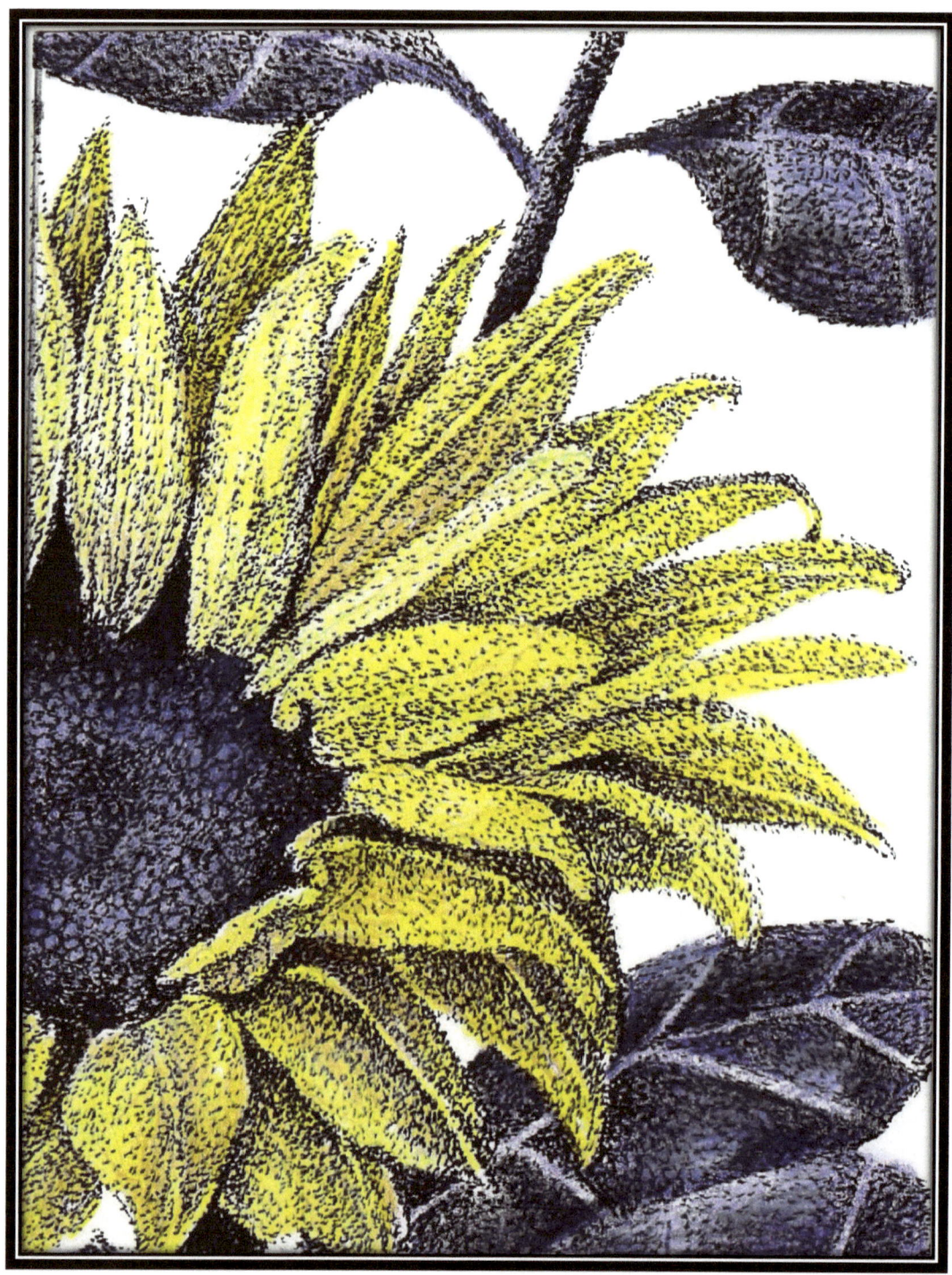

Triad

A triad color scheme means the artist has used three colors that are 1/3 away from each other on the color wheel. Also, black and white may be used.

I used red, yellow, and blue with black and white.

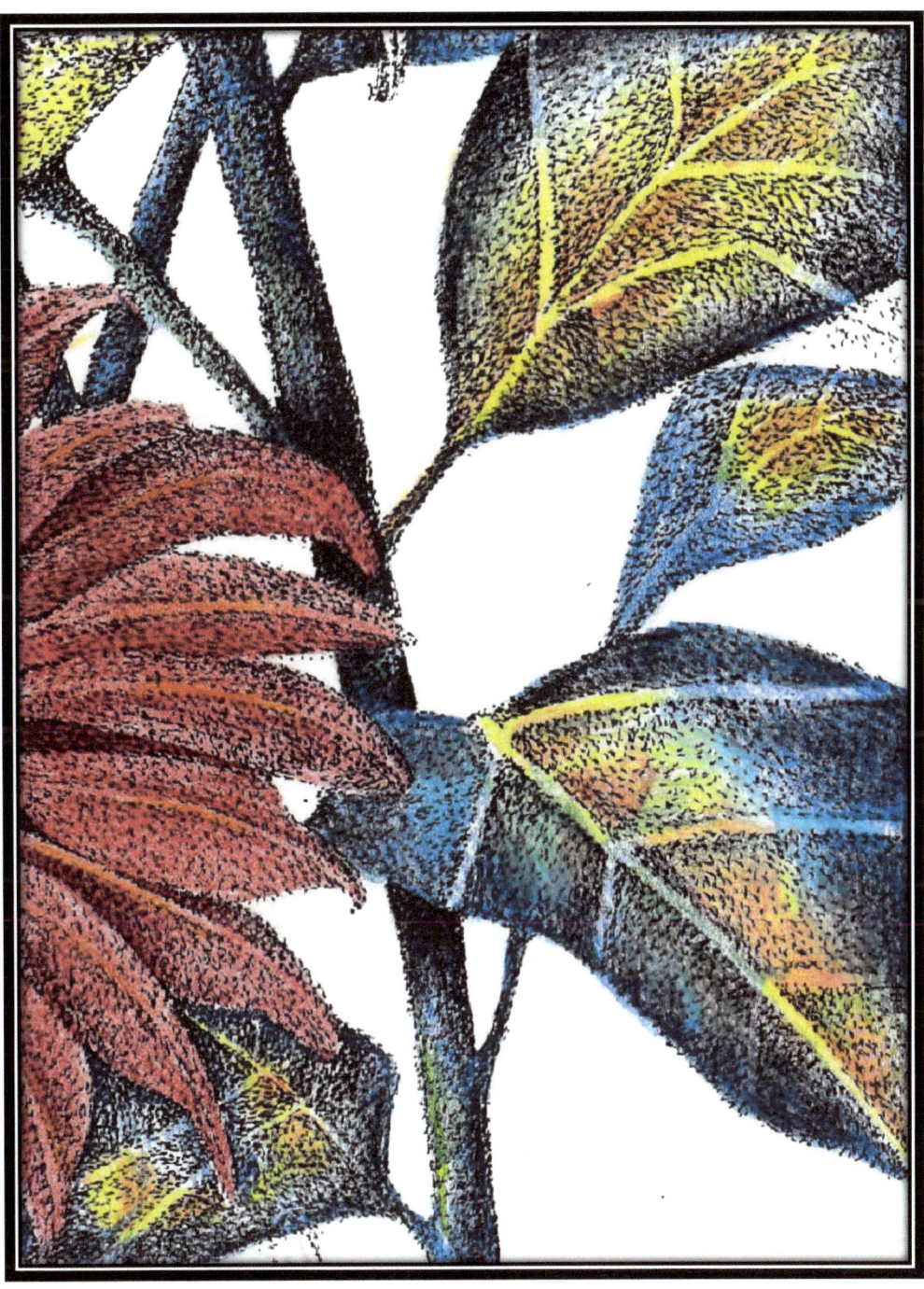

Now it's your turn...

I've included a colored example of each drawing as a version of how I completed each one. You should complete each drawing using your imagination.

Use your colored pencils to create contrast and three dimensionality. You'll do this with shading. There are two ways that I create shading. I employ pressure where I want the darker, more intense areas, and I layer colors over each other.

Examples:

Pressure

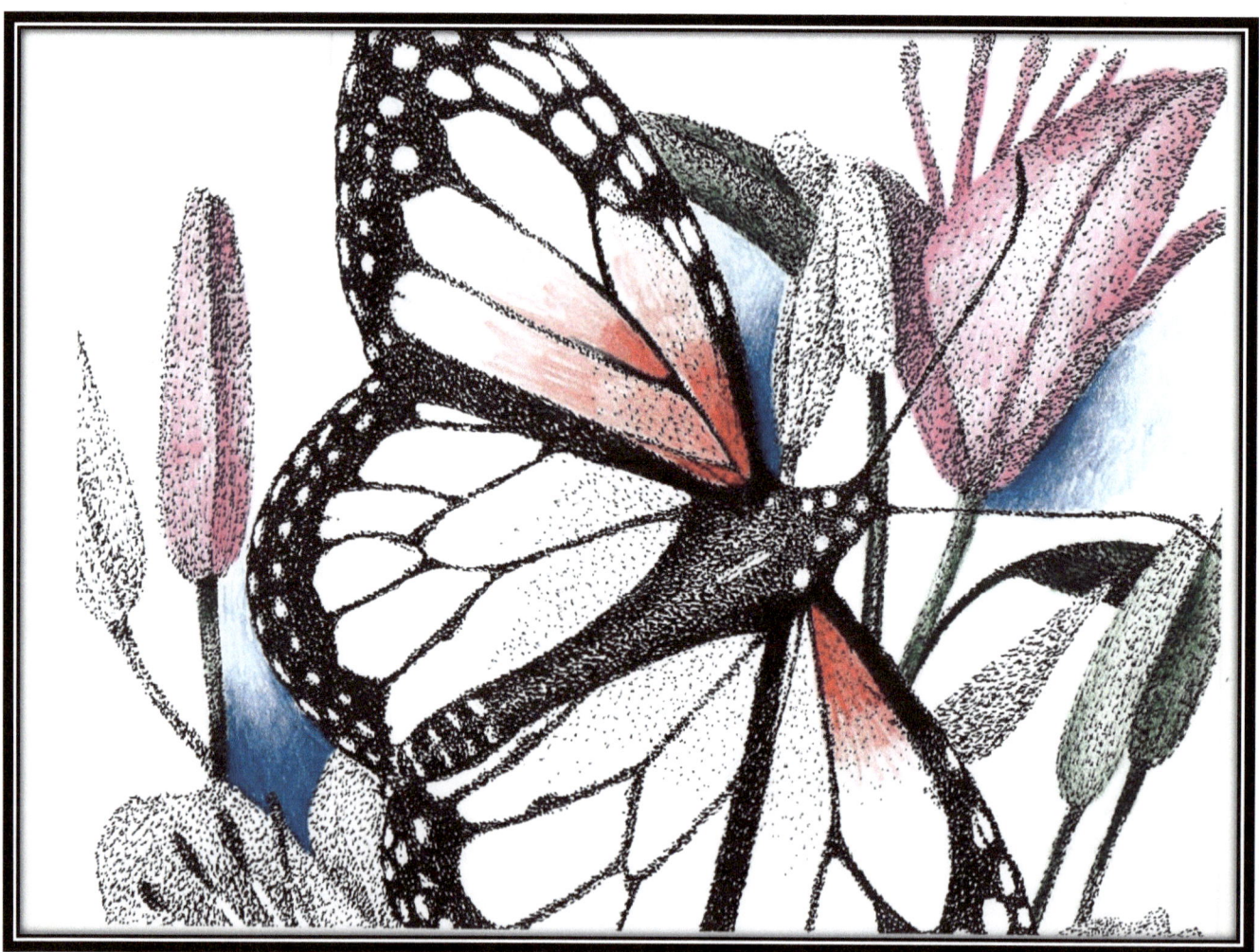

Layering

By layering, I mean the method an artist uses to add one color over another. You can use pencils to mix colors and values (making a color lighter or darker). Using the layering method will produce deeper, richer colors. You will notice a wider variety of hues.

Layering also enables the artist to shade objects and backgrounds, giving the illusion of three dimensionality.

I've deliberately left the example drawings unfinished, in hopes that you will practice layering before you begin work on the larger drawings.

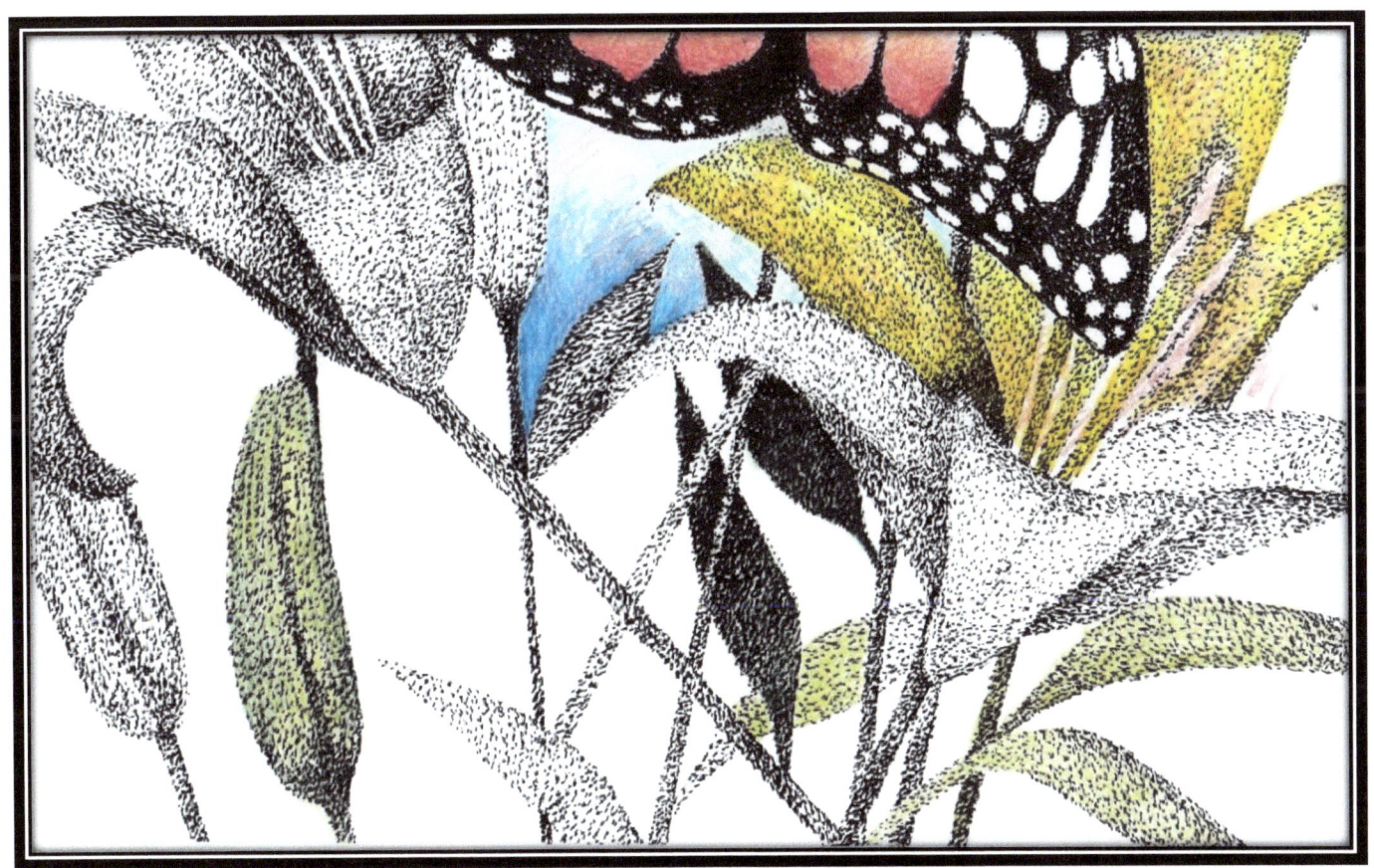

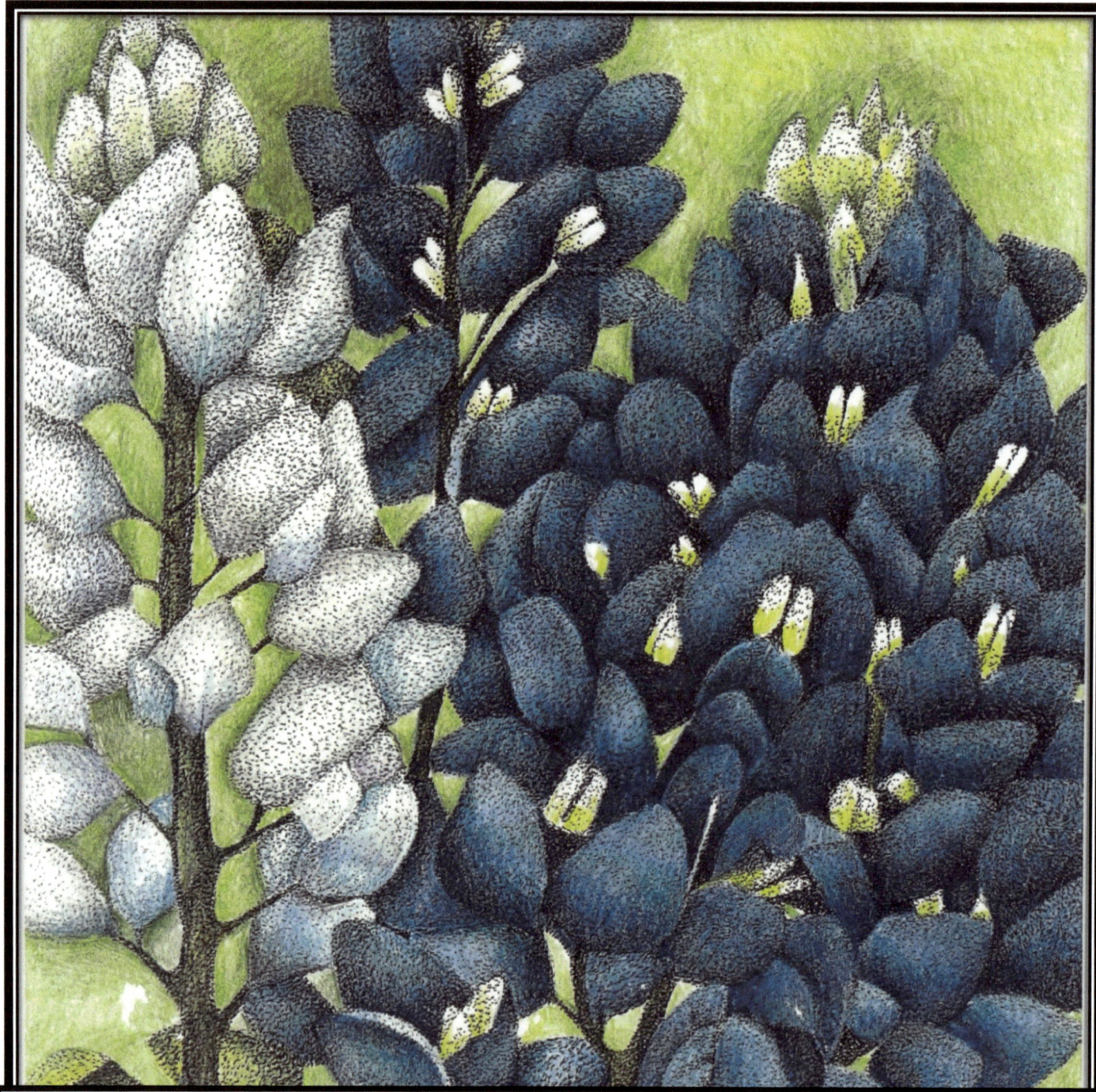

Bluebonnets

If you've ever come over a roadside hill and have seen a field of bluebonnets, you know what the fuss is about!

Their bright blue color against the green grass along a Texas roadside is truly a sight to behold. People often stop and photograph themselves and their loved ones surrounded by the beautiful blooms.

Bluebonnets received their name because of their resemblance to the bonnets pioneer women wore to protect their faces against the sun.

Bluebonnets became the Texas state flower in 1901. They bloom from March to May and do best in dry soil. They are a cherished part of Texas heritage and said to represent bravery, sacrifice, and honor.

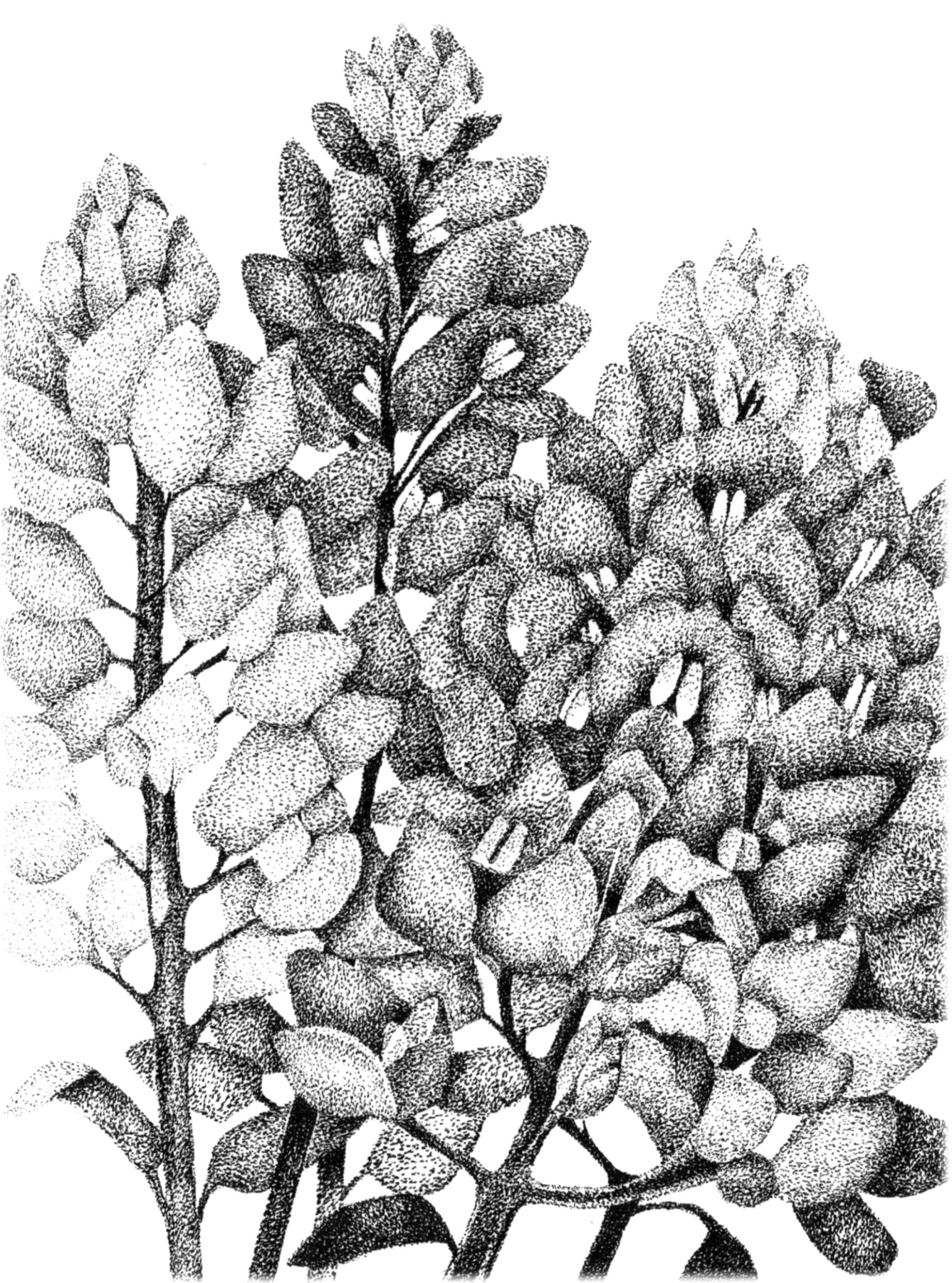

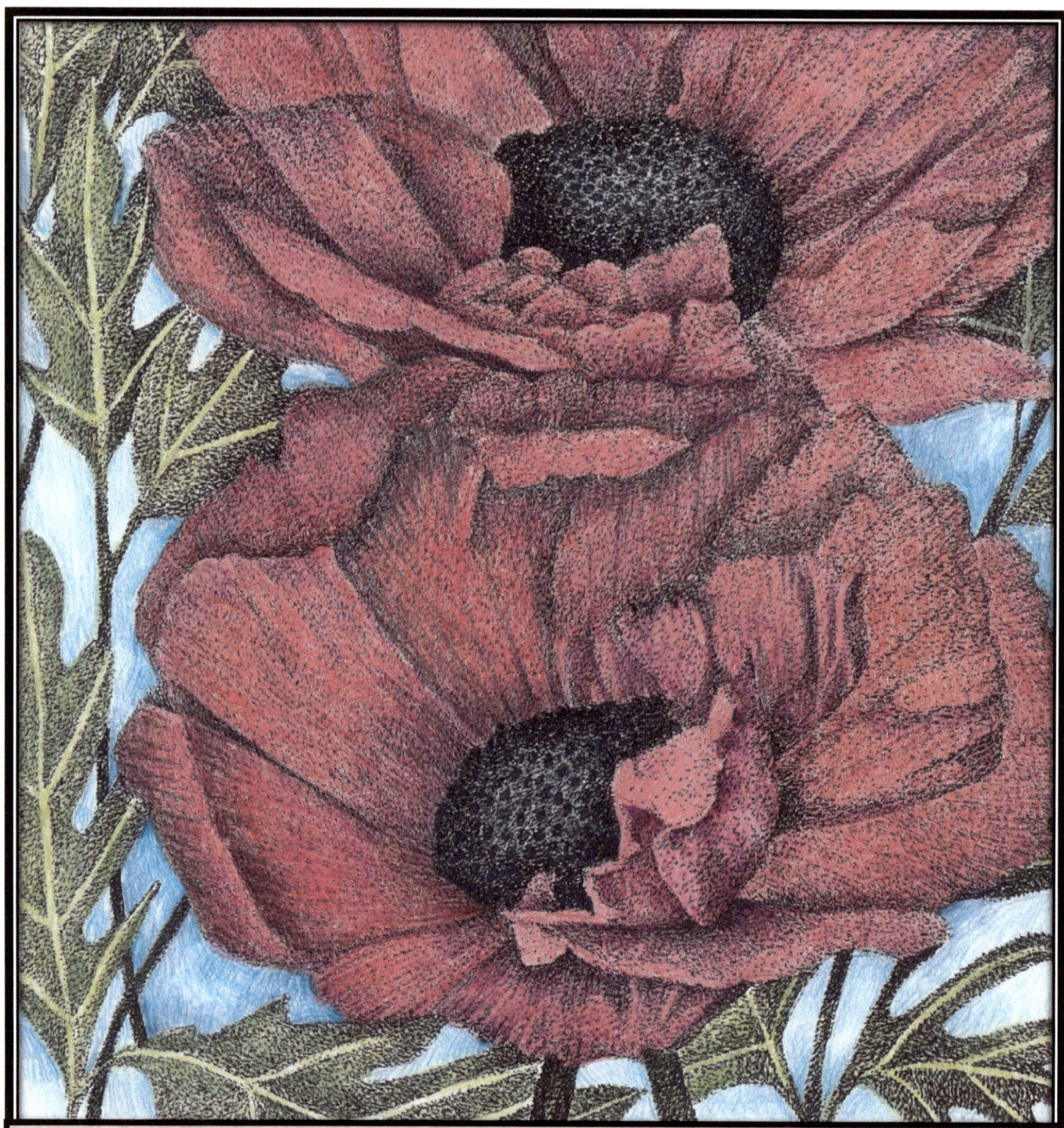

Poppies

Poppies have inspired people for hundreds of years. They have taken on many symbols. Grief and loss were most eloquently expressed by poppies as a symbol of World War One. After four brutal years of war, poppies were planted on battlefields and they come back year after year as a symbol of hope.

Poppies also have a darker reputation. They are well known as an ingredient in the production of heroin and oxycodone. In small doses the poppy is beneficial. We use poppy seeds in a variety of our food, including toppings on bagels and in muffins. Today poppies are worn and given as gifts as a symbol of remembrance and hope for the future.

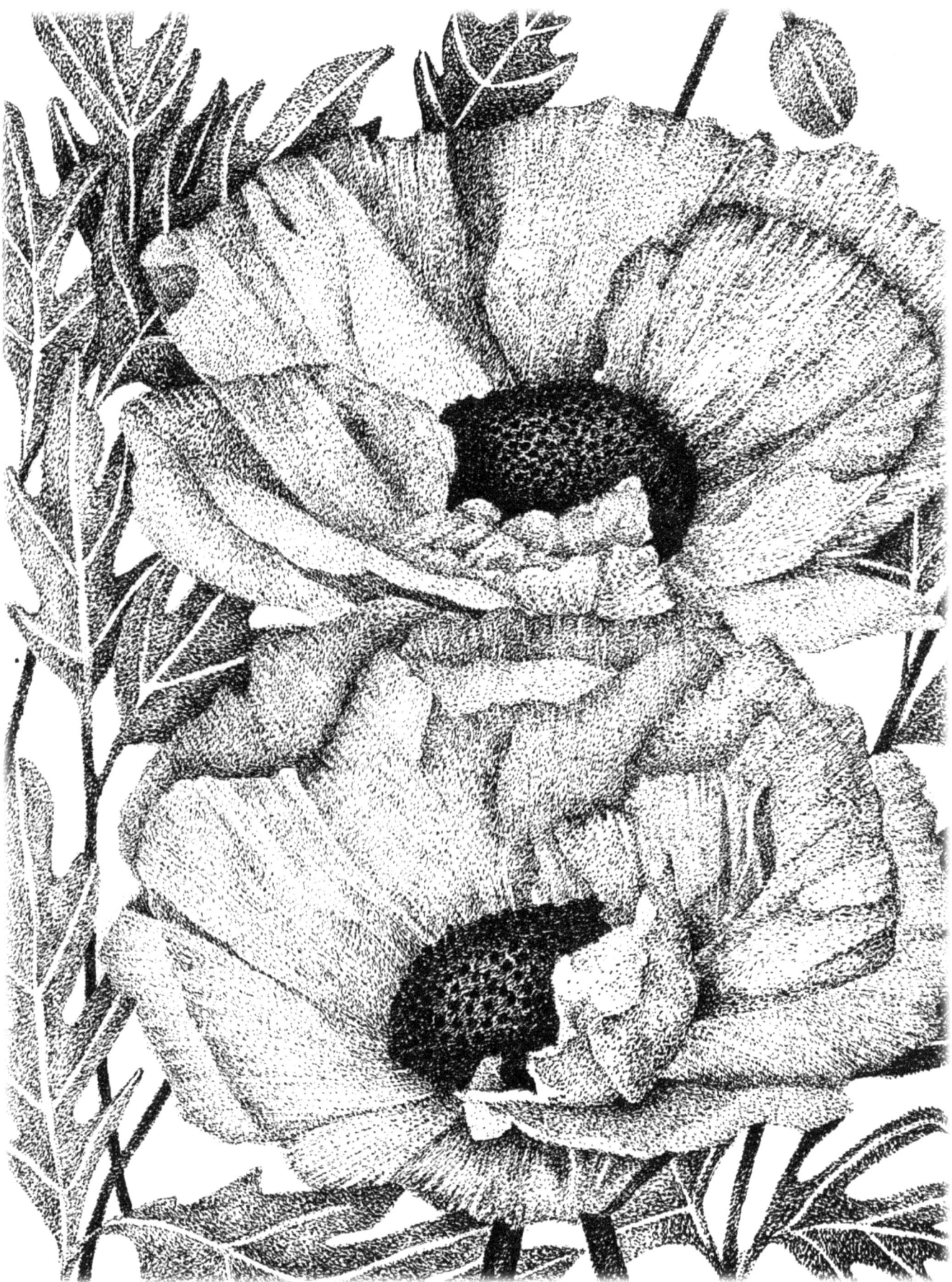

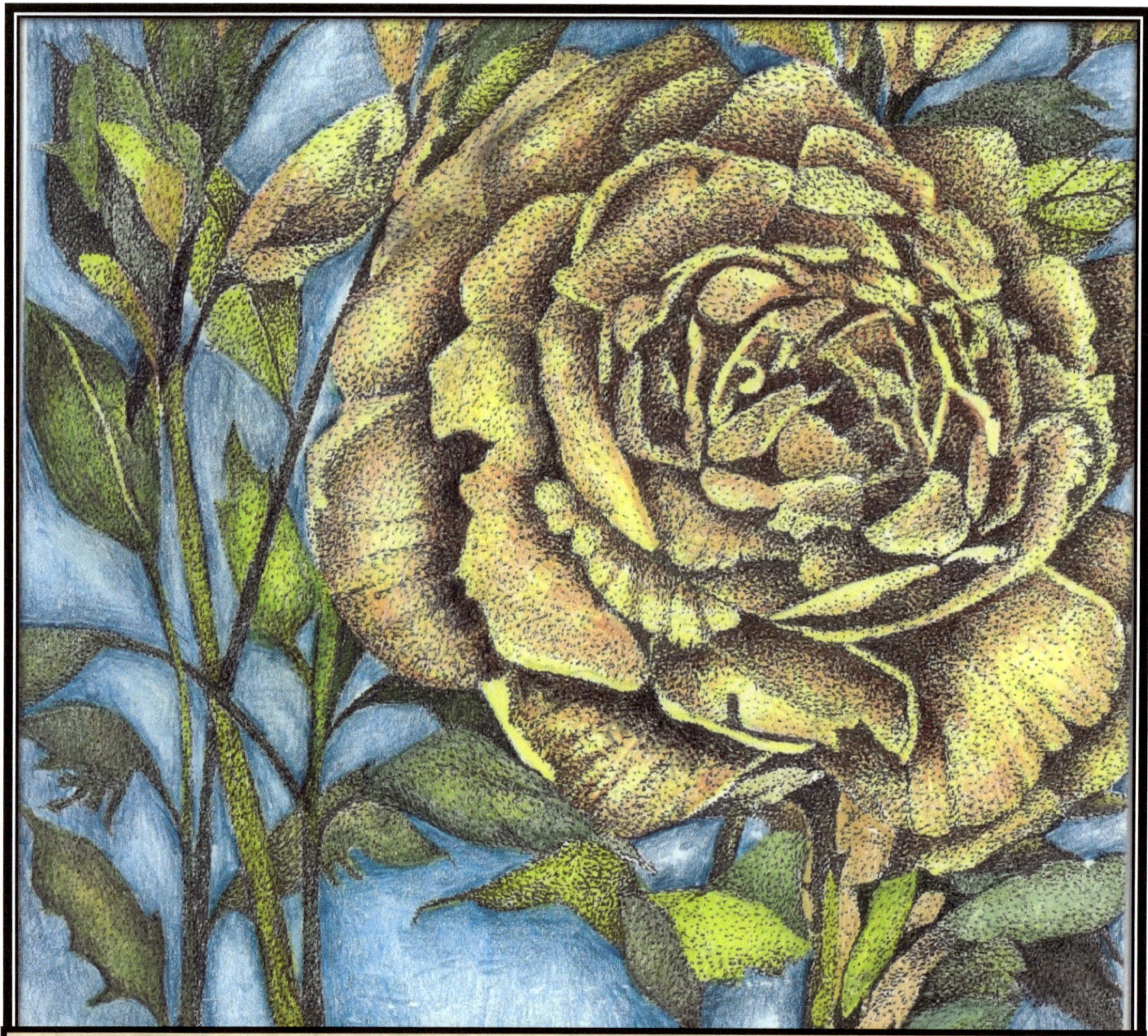

Rose

What an amazing flower is the beautiful rose! All over the world, the rose is often considered the most beautiful and popular flower. In the United Sates, eighty-five per cent of people asked listed the rose as their favorite flower. The rose is the national flower of 10 countries, including the U.S.

Red roses are the traditional gift on Valentine's Day, symbolizing love. There is even the Rose Parade, which began in 1890 and consists of floats covered entirely with flowers. It is traditionally held on New Years Day in Pasadena, California. While June is national Rose Month, roses are treasured all year.

George Washington was a rose breeder. He bred a special rose named after his mother; the "Mary Washington" rose. Other roses named after American presidents were the Lincoln rose, the Reagan rose, and the John F. Kennedy rose.

Over 4,000 songs are dedicated to roses, including the "Yellow Rose of Texas.'" The yellow rose is said to be a symbol of cheerfulness and friendship

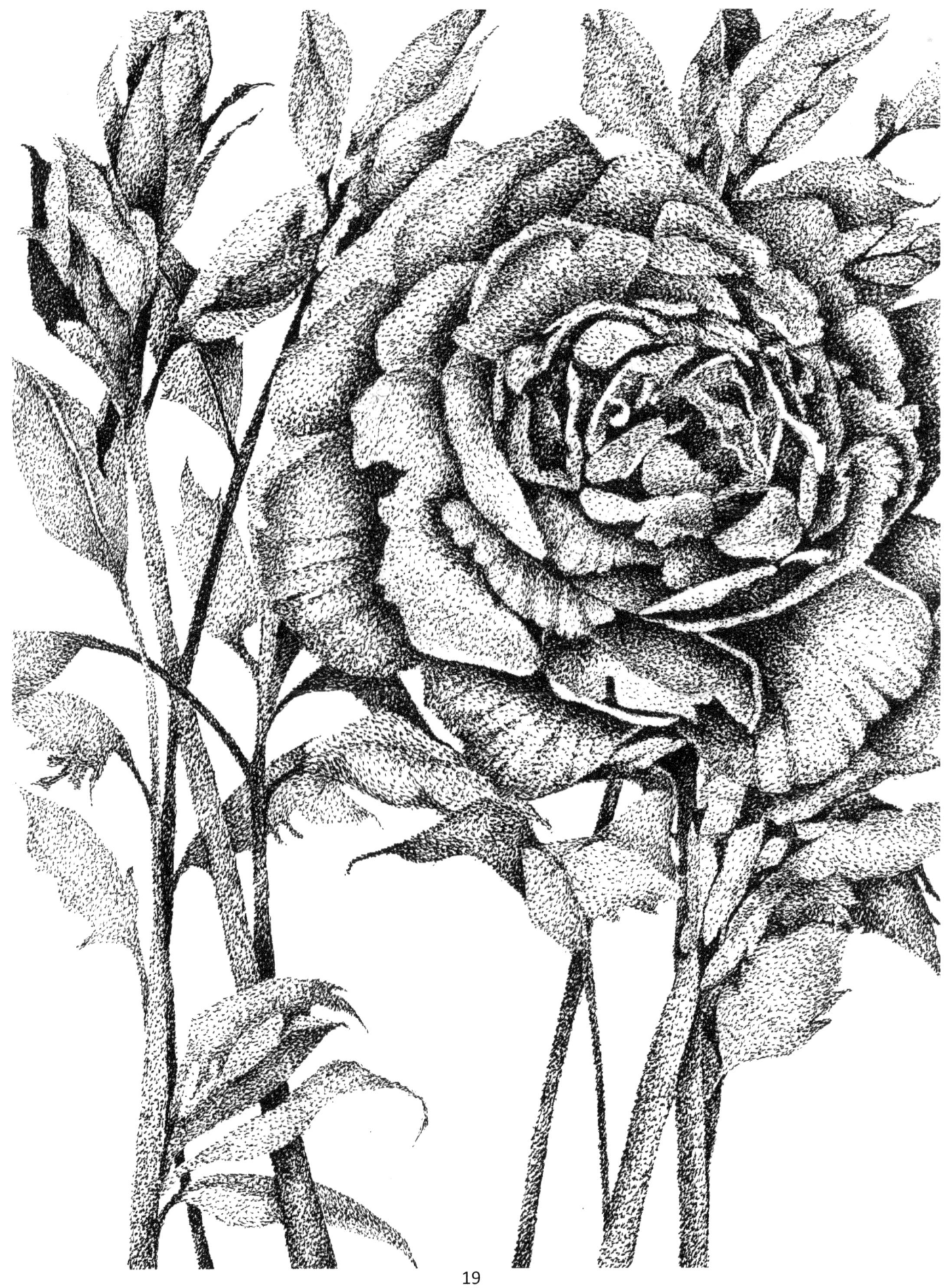

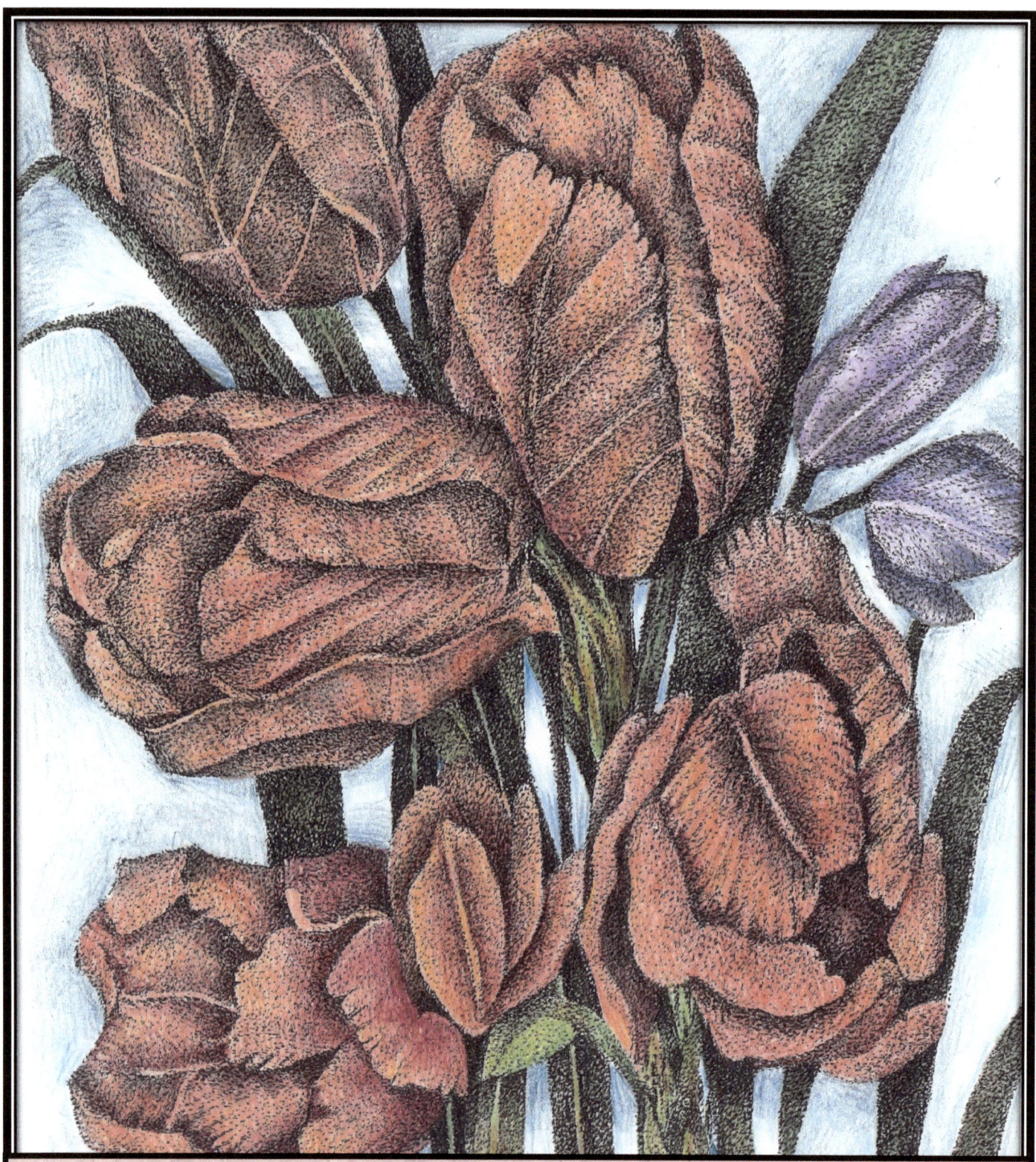

Tulips

Tulips are widely popular around the world. People love them for their large intensely colored blooms and their graceful long stems and leaves.

Spring is the prime season for tulip viewing and there are numerous tulip viewings and festivals around the world. In May, the Canadian Tulip Festival is held in Ottaway, Canada. It is said to be the world's largest tulip festival with over 1,000,000 tulips featured. This festival attracts 650,000 visitors each year.

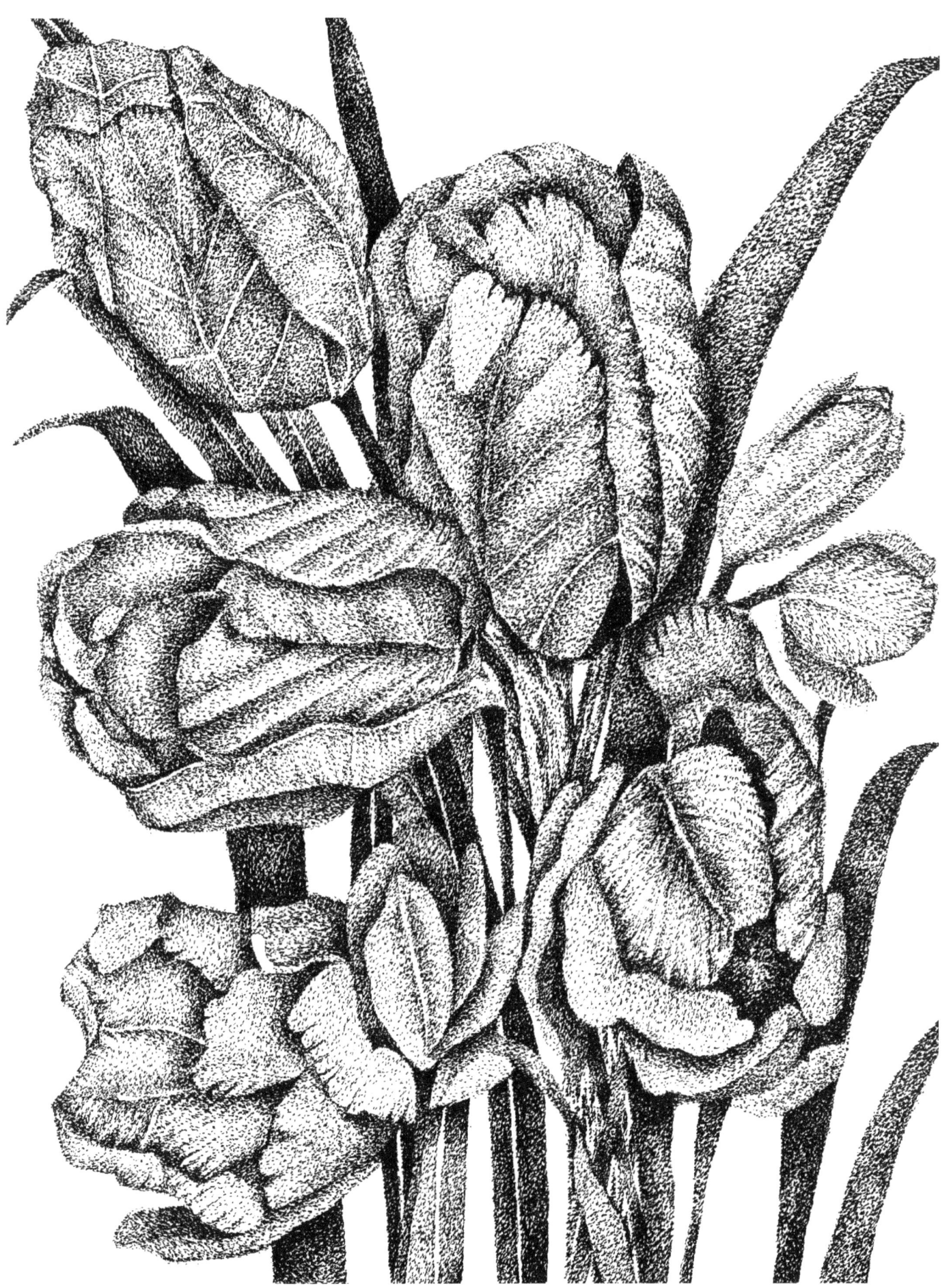

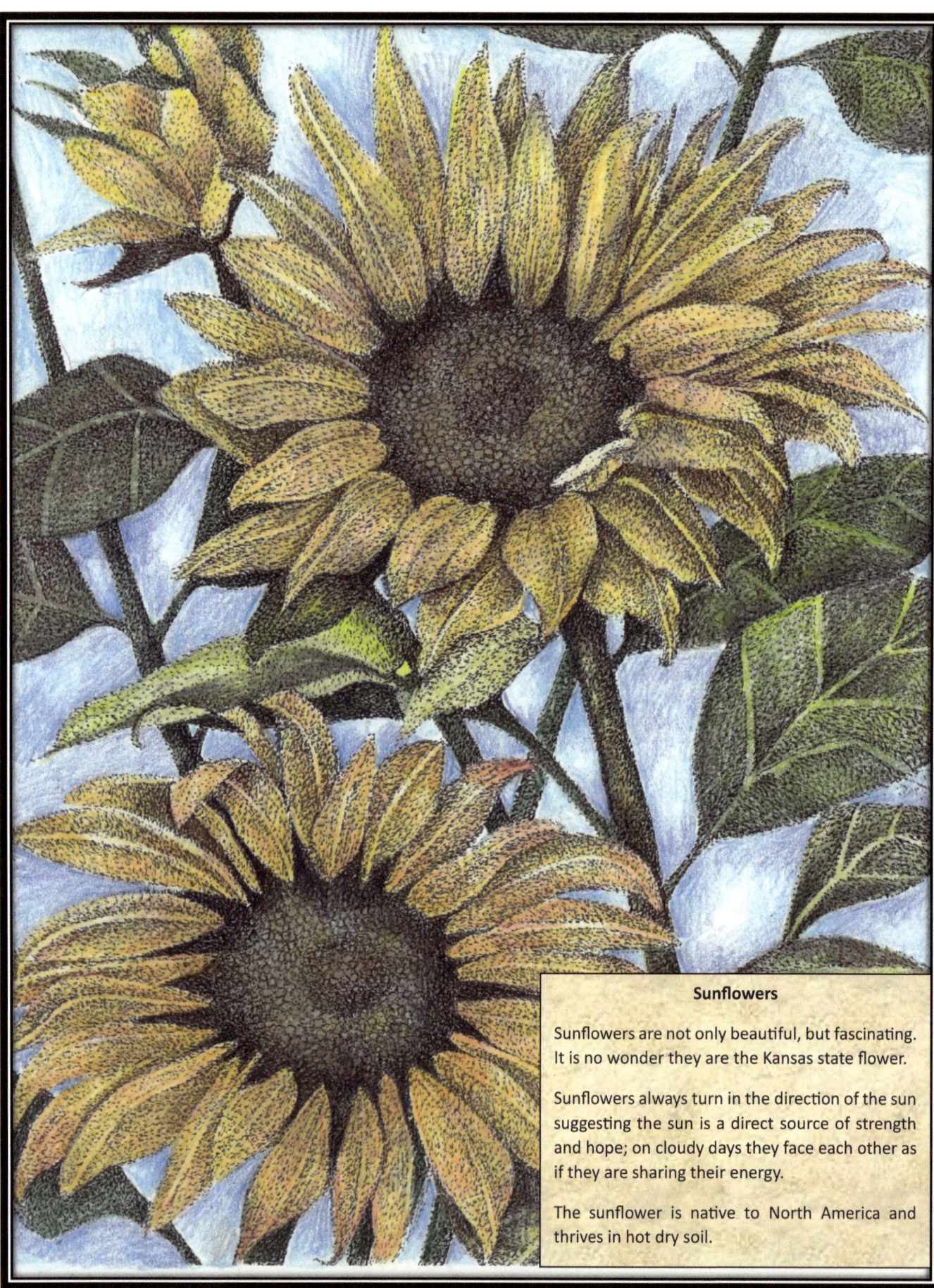

Sunflowers

Sunflowers are not only beautiful, but fascinating. It is no wonder they are the Kansas state flower.

Sunflowers always turn in the direction of the sun suggesting the sun is a direct source of strength and hope; on cloudy days they face each other as if they are sharing their energy.

The sunflower is native to North America and thrives in hot dry soil.

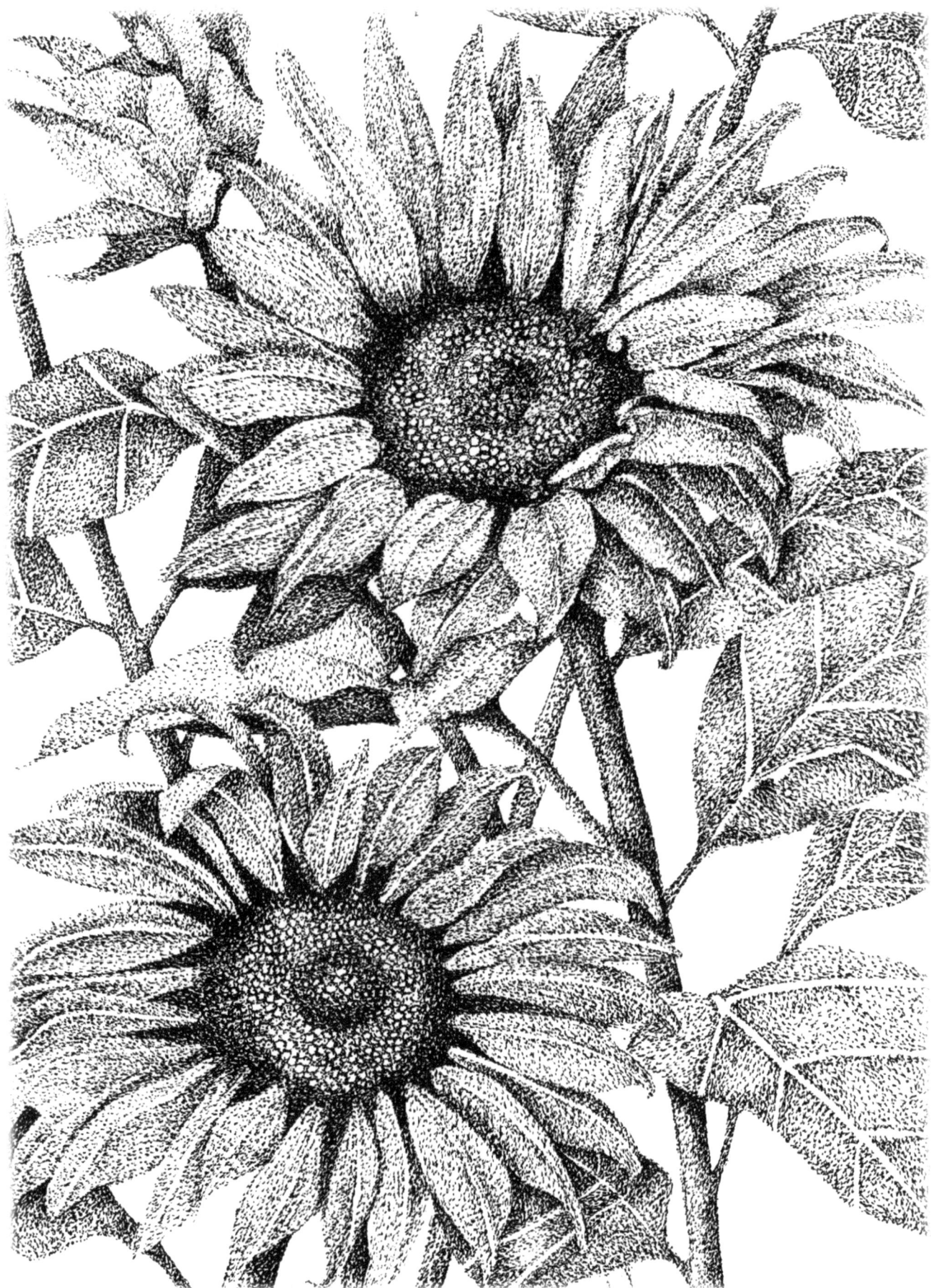

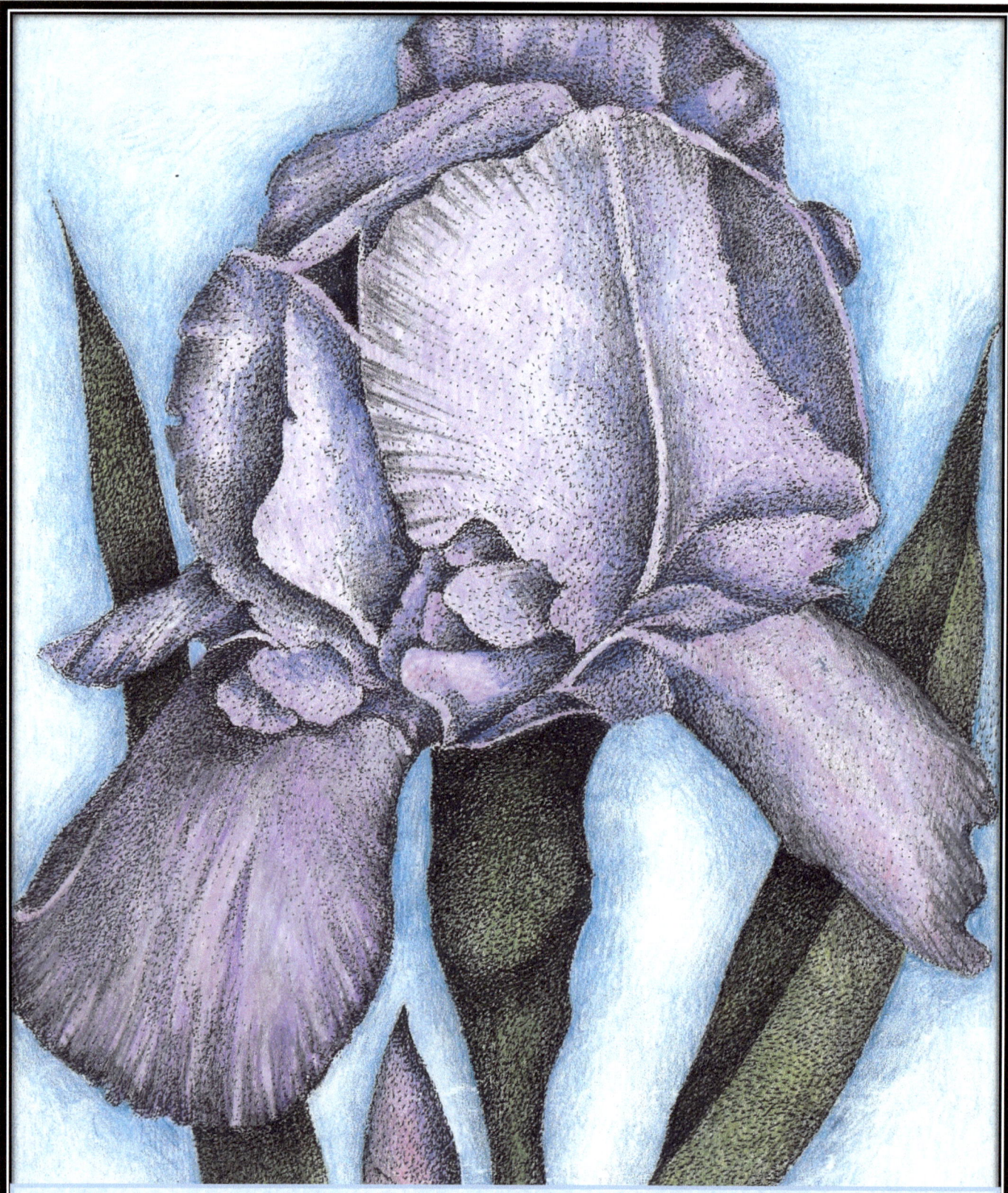

Iris

It's no wonder the French adopted the iris as their national symbol. The fleur-de-lis takes its design from the iris. Two of the most common colors of the iris are blue and purple, colors which symbolize peace and tranquility.

The beauty of the iris reminds us to take a moment to relax and concentrate on developing inner peace. They remind us that inspiration can come from unexpected sources.

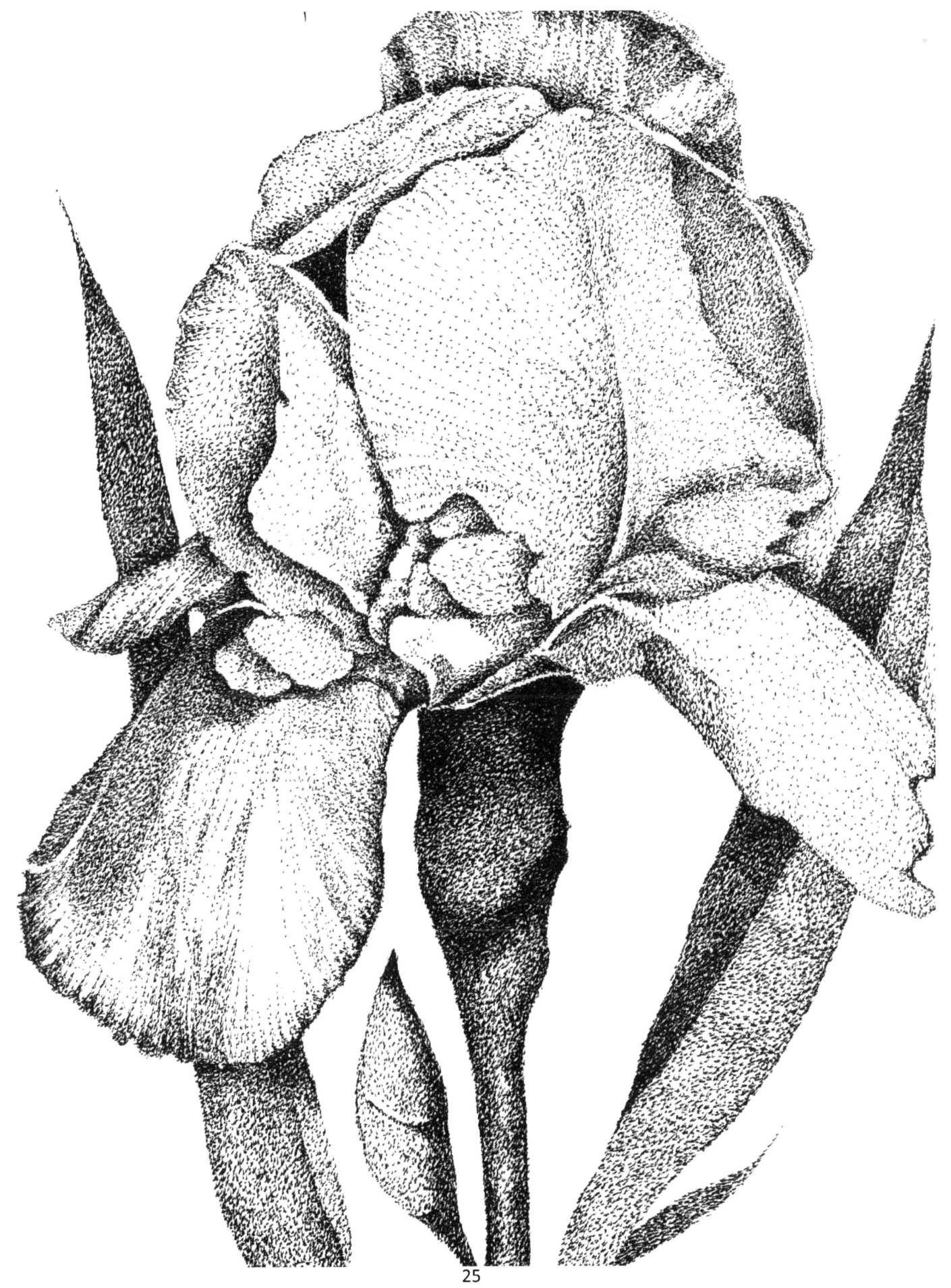

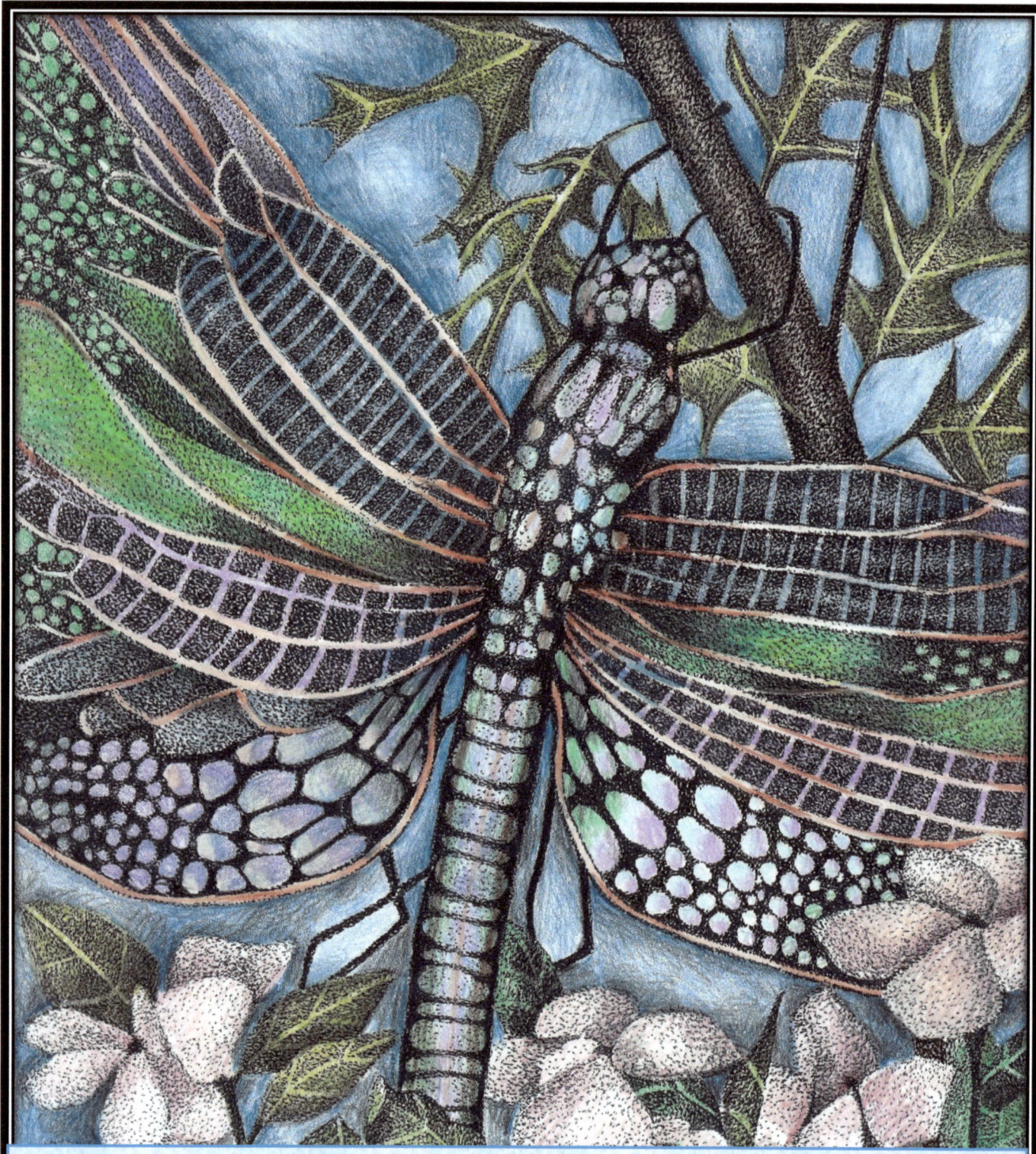

Dragonflies

It's hard to take your eyes off a dragonfly. Their beauty and effortless flight capture our imagination, resembling floating fairy-like creatures. Color glows from their tiny bodies. Their wings are like shimmery lace. Their long colorful bodies are covered with glowing colors and intricate patterns. Dragonflies are an artist's dream, but it's difficult to duplicate their natural beauty.

Dragonflies can be found throughout the world, but they thrive in mild, watery climates. They spend most of their lives around wetland areas, feasting on mosquitoes, butterflies and other dragonflies. Their lifespan is two weeks to two months. Amazingly, dragonfly fossils have been found which date back 3,000,000 years.

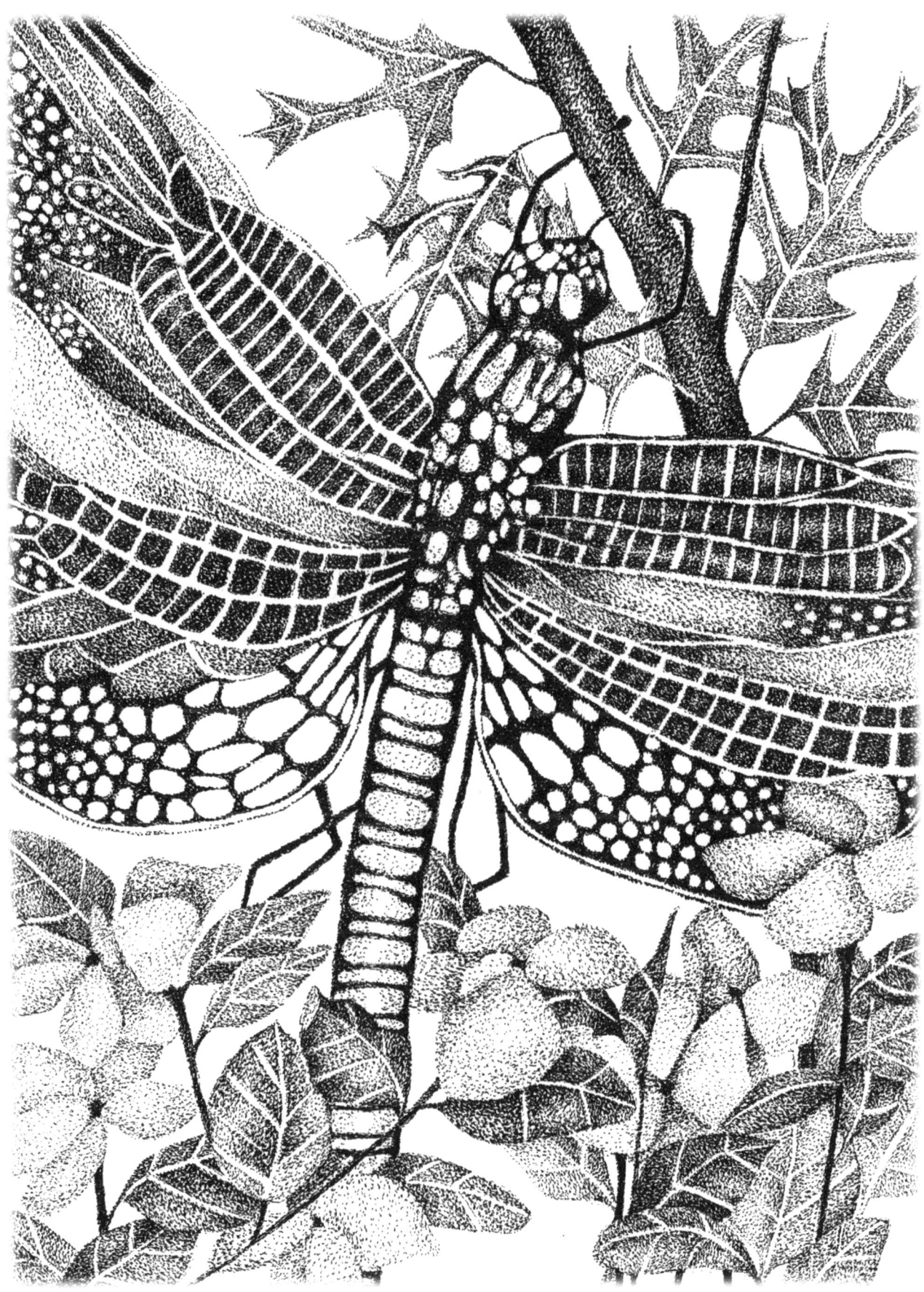

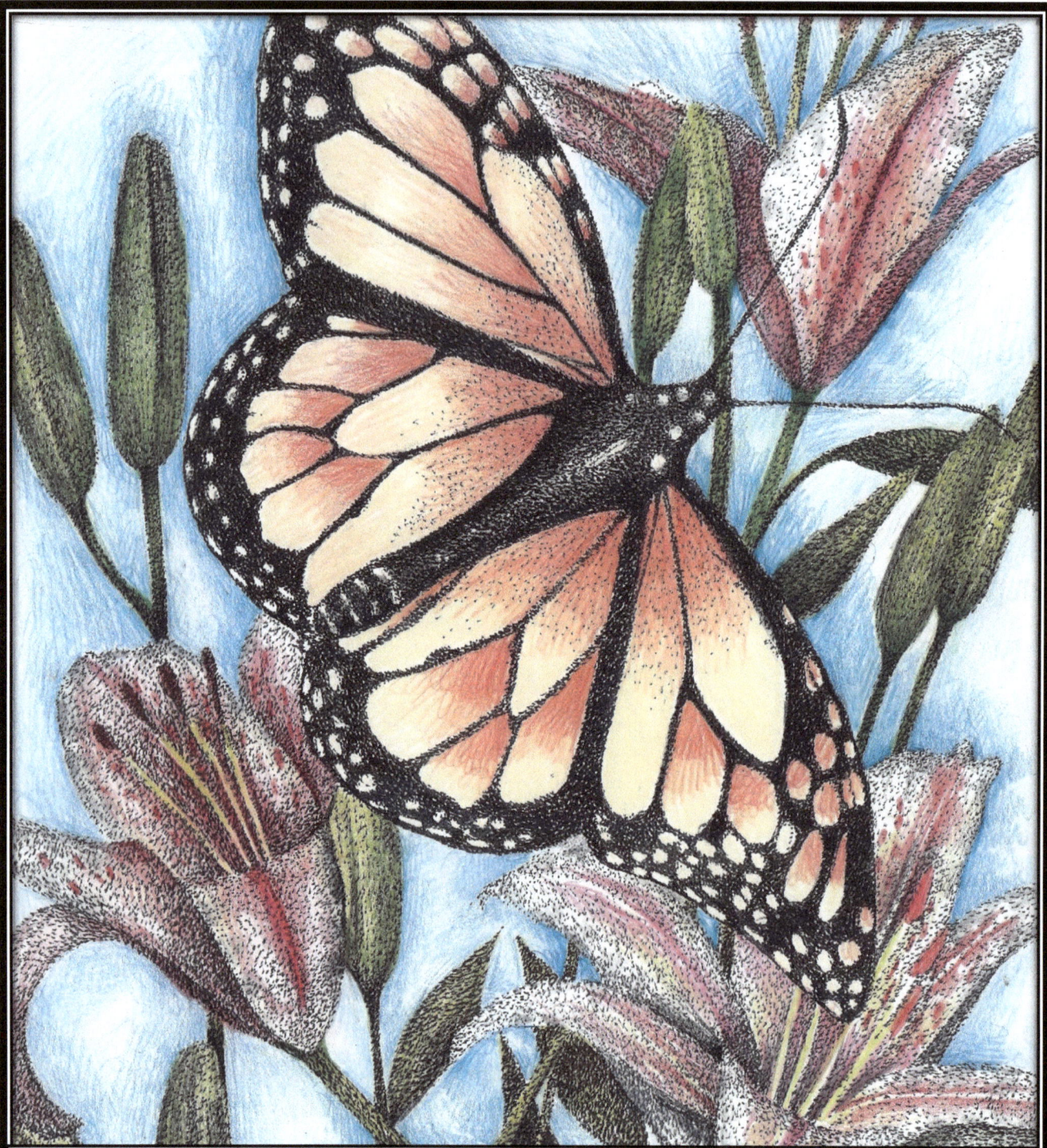

Monarch Butterflies

Monarch butterflies can be found all over the world. Fans of the monarch are attracted to them because of their bright colors, graceful flight and delicate detail. They're easy to spot with their bright orange coloring and detailed veining in their wings. Although monarchs have a short lifespan, they are hardy enough to make their migratory journeys of up to 3,000 miles every spring and fall. It only takes two to six weeks for a monarch caterpillar to become a butterfly.

Monarchs need one specific plant to survive, the milk weed. Females lay their tiny eggs on the underside of the leaves of this plant. In storing the toxic juices from milkweed in their bodies, they are protected from predators.

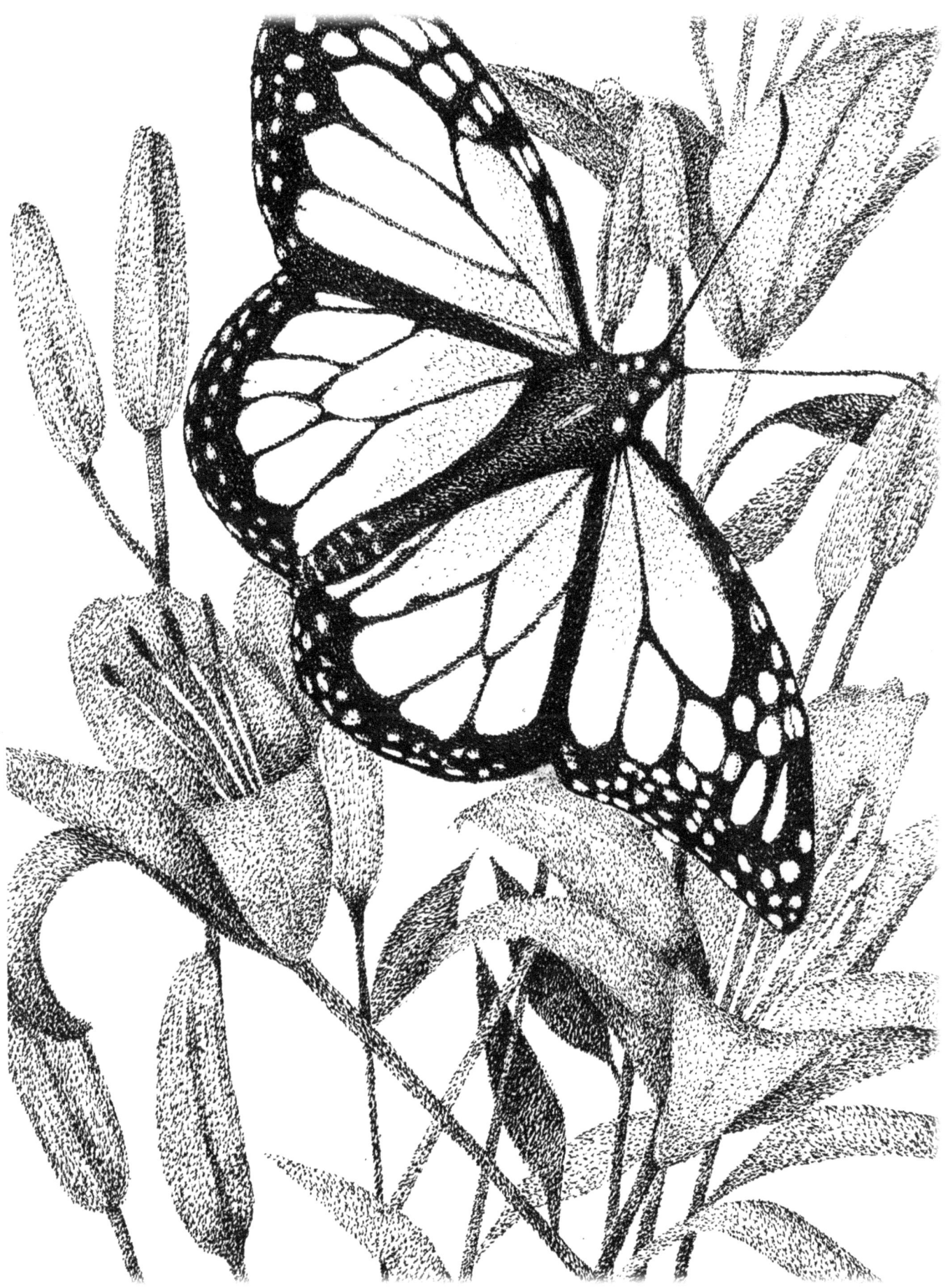

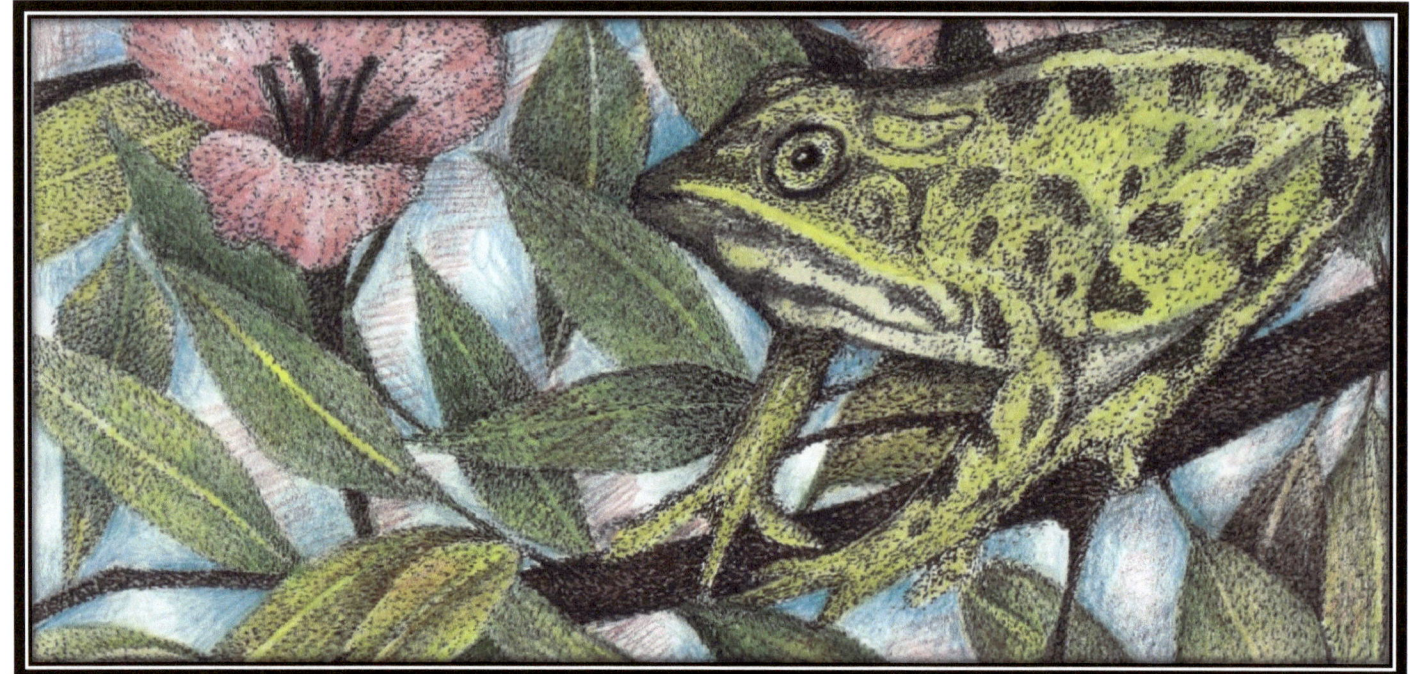

Tree Frogs

At night they sound like barking dogs in the trees. When describing the tree frog, one should mention shiny colors. The top of its body is usually a bright yellow green which gradually blends into a dark olive green on its lower side. Its stomach can be white, brownish white or pinkish. Its eyes are usually a pale gold.

A tree frog is any of 800 species of frogs who spend most of his life in the trees. The ends of a tree frog's toes feature large disks that aid in climbing trees. Tree frog females are larger than males. Females average four inches in length compared to males at three inches. Some females lay their eggs on tree leaves overhanging water while others lay their eggs in the water.

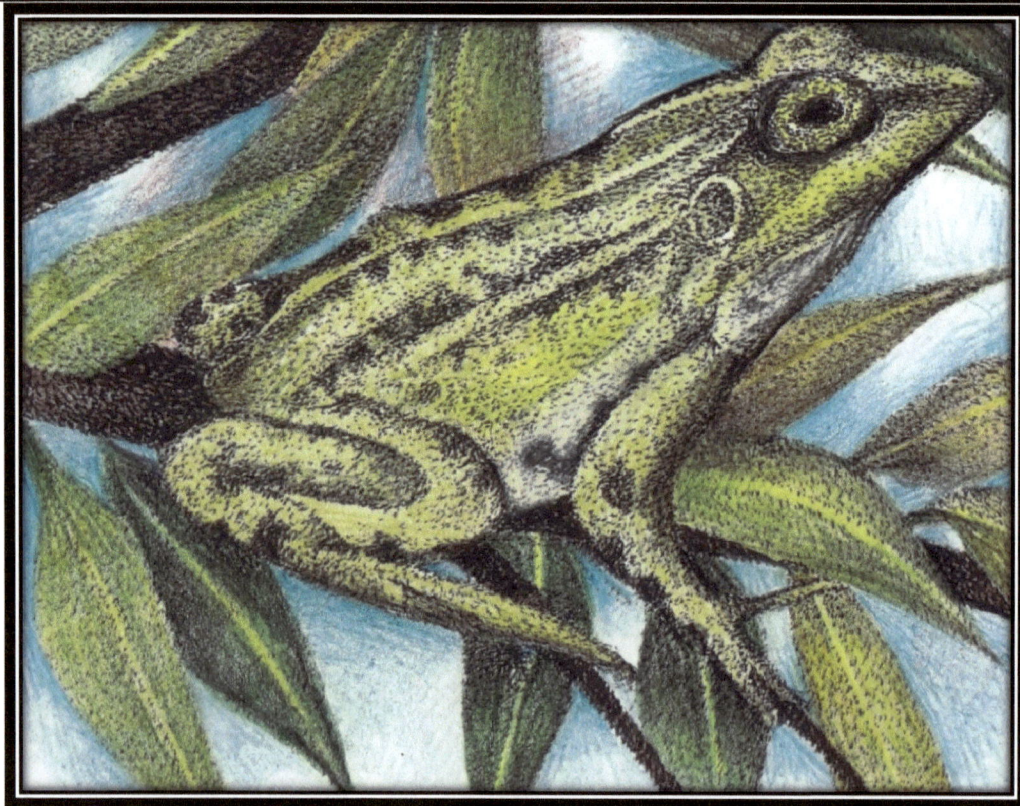

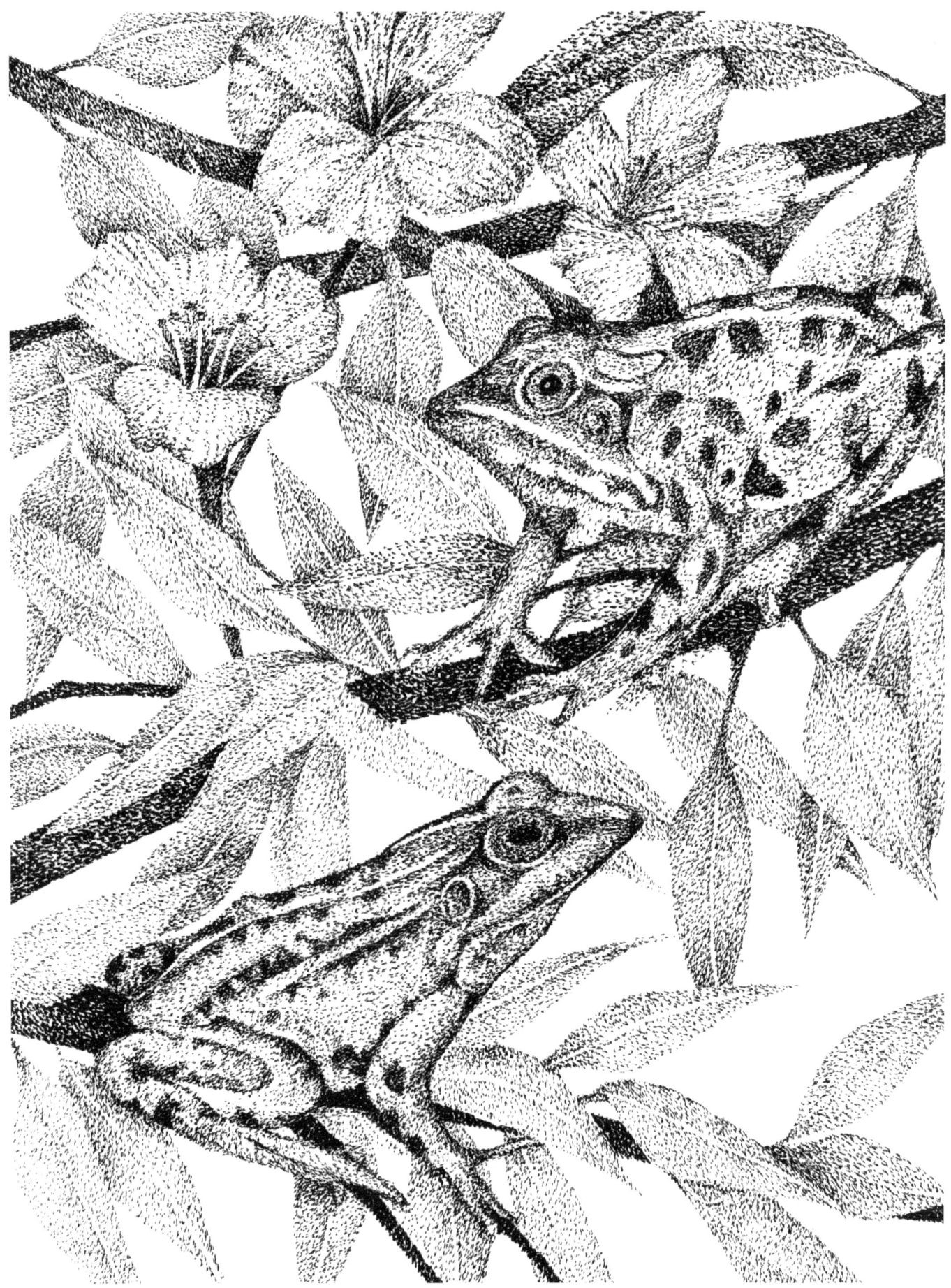

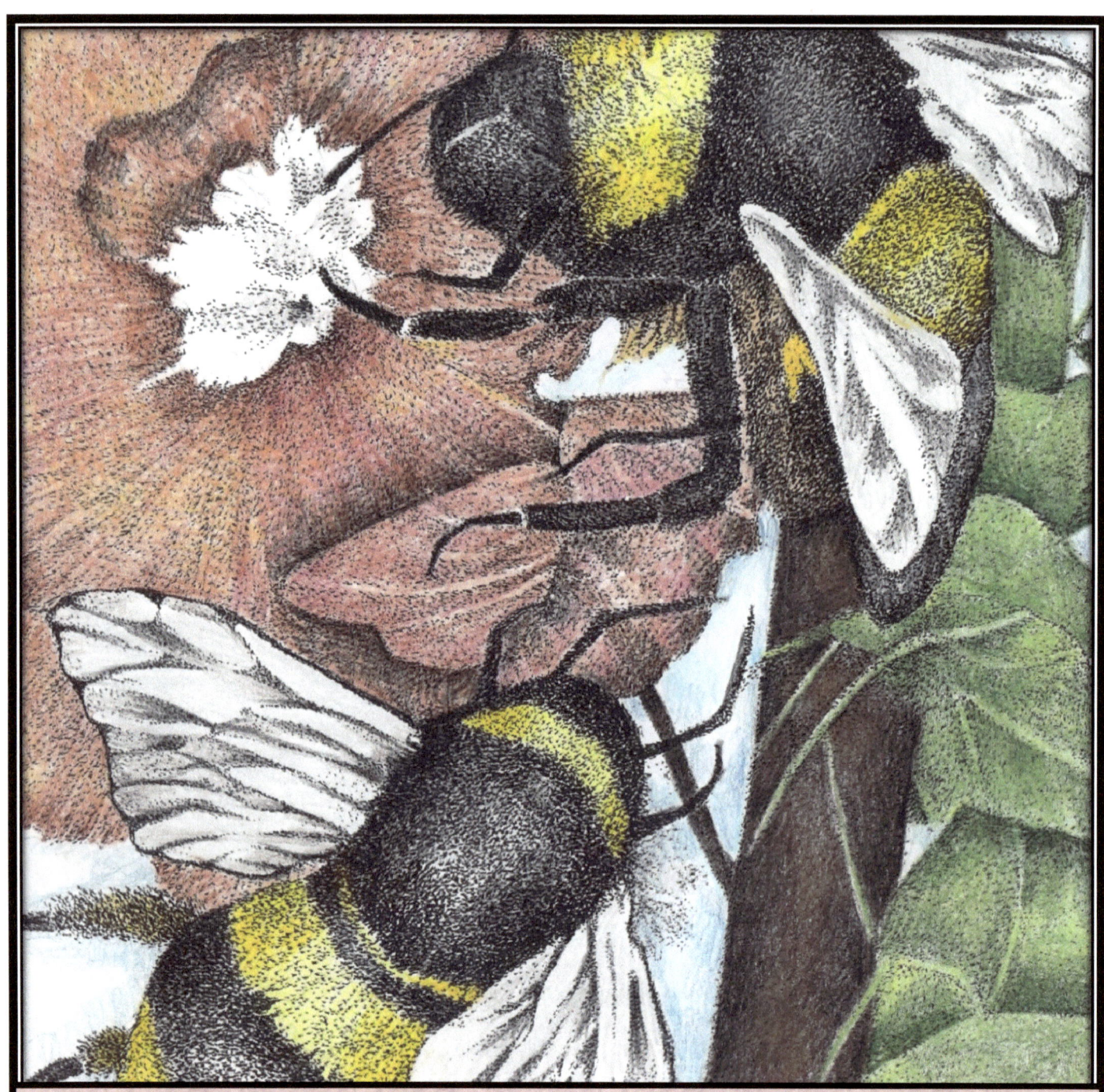

Honey Bees

If you've ever heard a buzzing noise while in your garden, you have probably been close to a honey bee. Stop and watch one of the hardest working insects on earth. Colonies are groups of bees that live and work together and the hive is their home. Female worker bees are in charge of pollinating most of the plants on earth. They are also the honey makers of the hive. There is only one queen bee in a hive and she can lay up to 2,000 eggs a day. The queen is a fertilized adult female who runs the entire colony.

Recently people have become concerned about the dangerous possibility that the bees' existence is threatened. Without these important insects, the world's food supply could be in serious trouble.

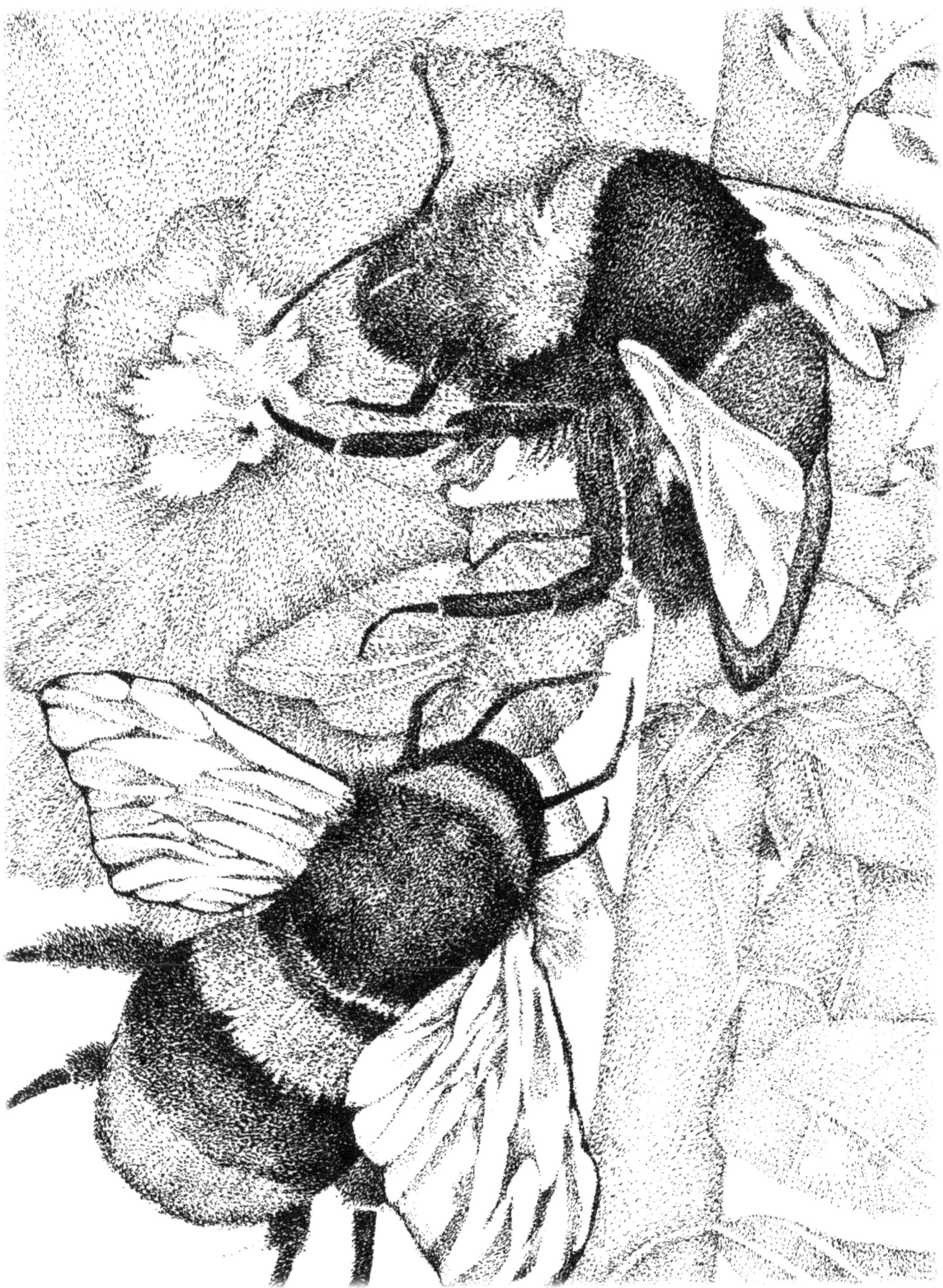

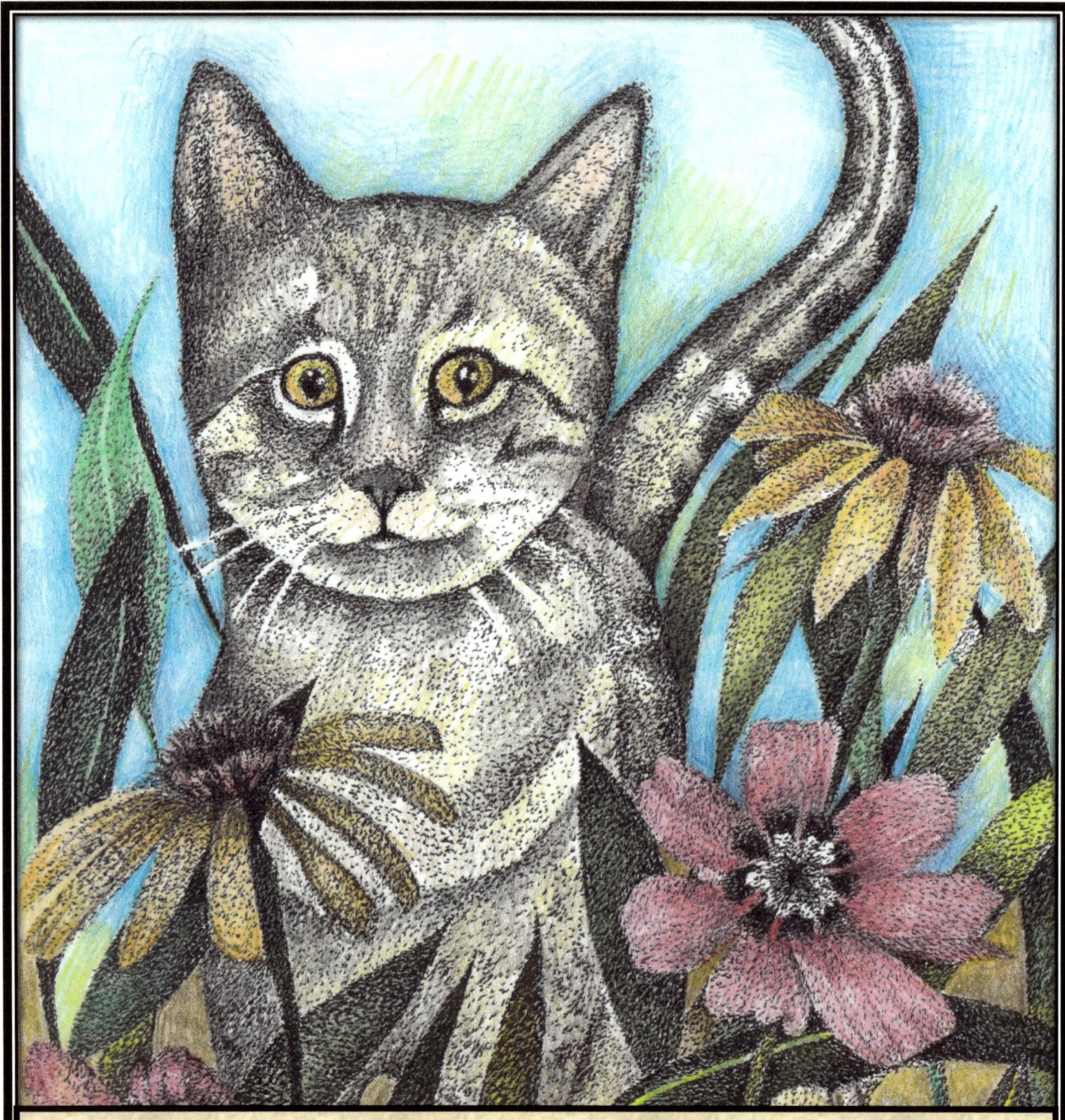

Cats

Cats and humans have had relationships dating back thousands of years. Families all over the world consider their cats valued members of the family. Cats need independence and routine to thrive. They can live happily in groups with other cats or humans but are also able to live alone. They will often avoid conflict in unfamiliar situations and hide from strangers. When hiding is not possible, they will either freeze or actively defend themselves.

Cats have exceptional hearing. They are sensitive to high pitched sounds and other loud noises. Their sense of smell is 10,000 times better than humans.

Happy relationships with other creatures are not always possible. Cats often choose to hunt small prey. They are, after all, related to tigers!

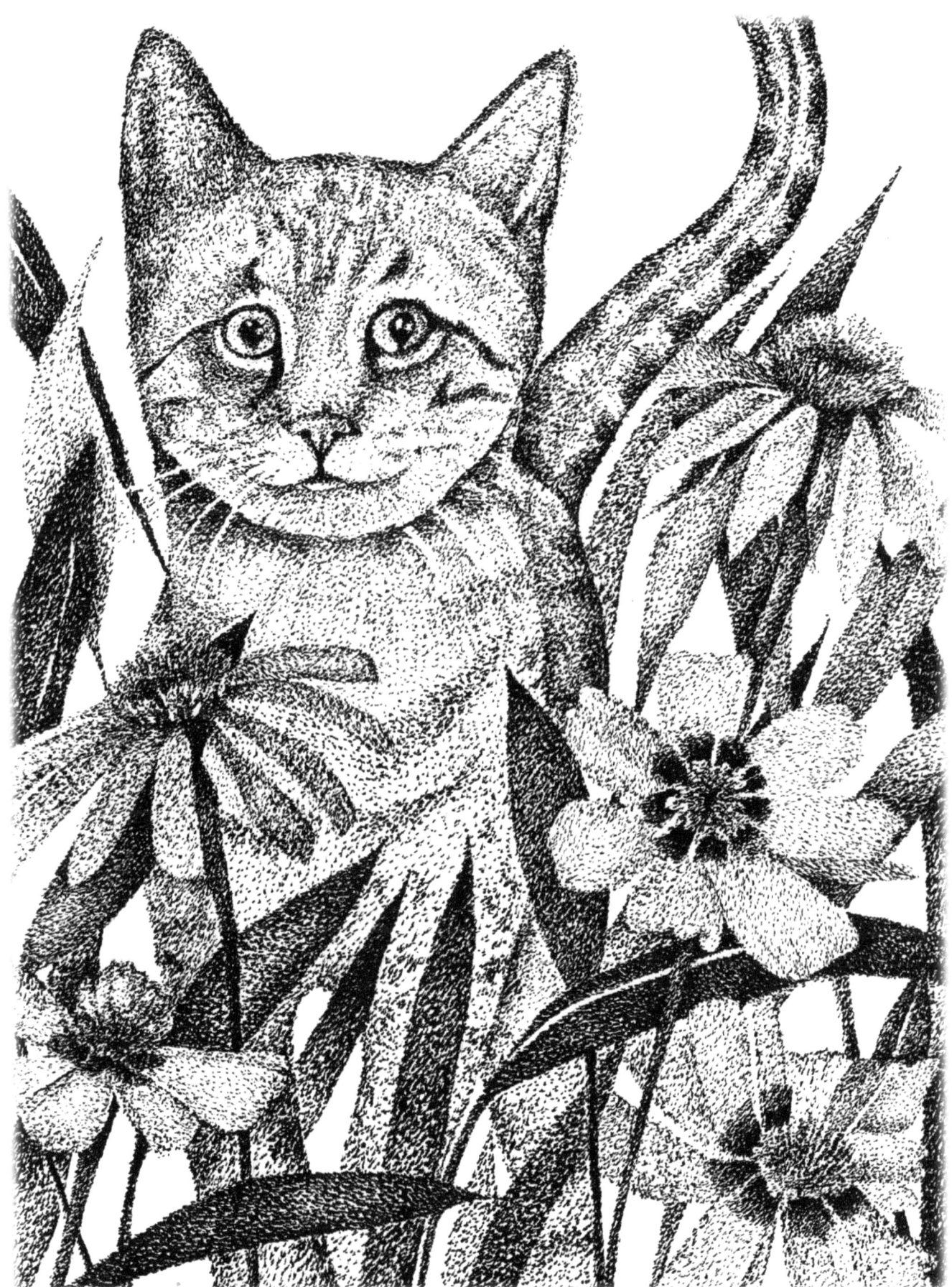

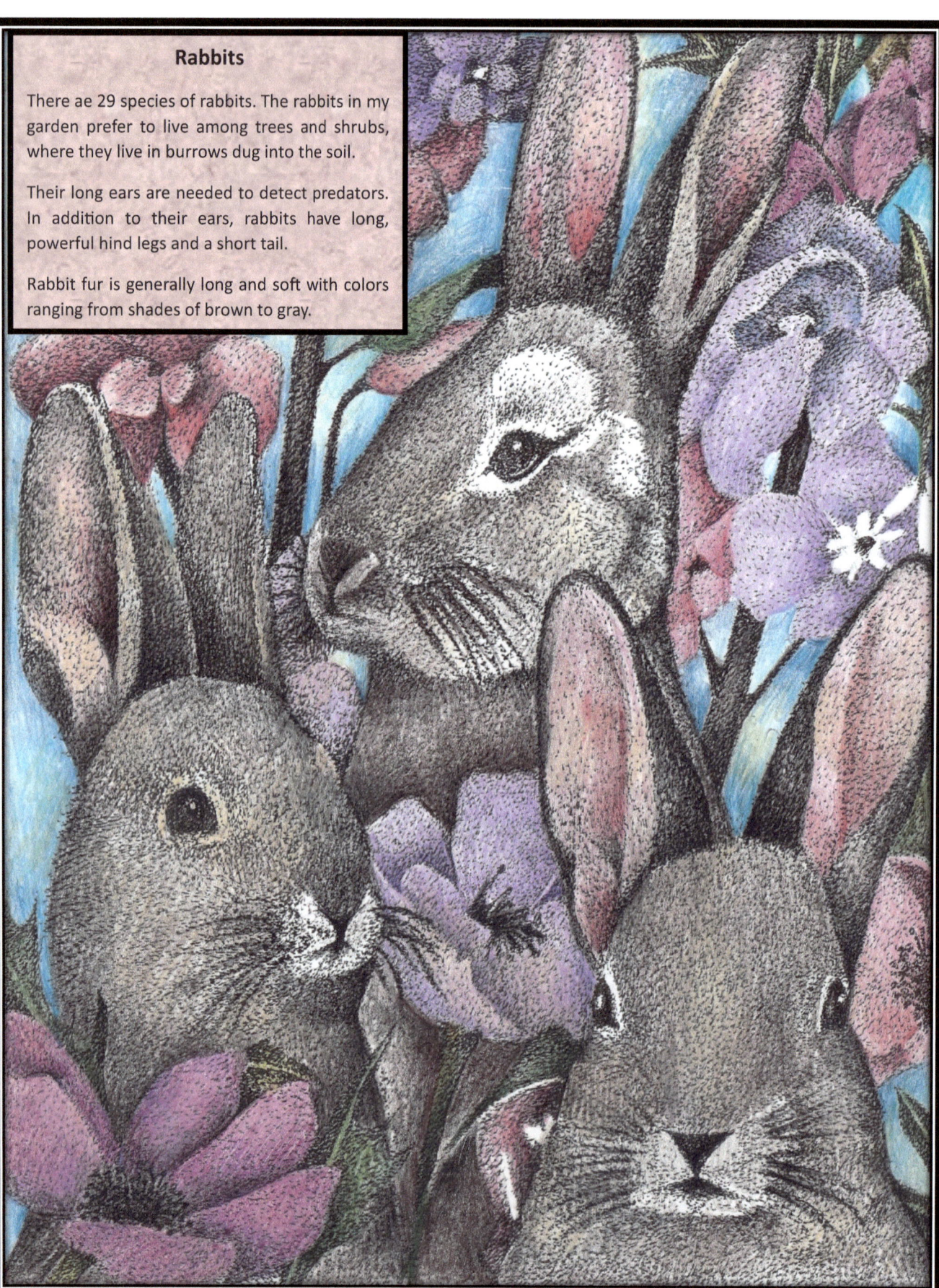

Rabbits

There ae 29 species of rabbits. The rabbits in my garden prefer to live among trees and shrubs, where they live in burrows dug into the soil.

Their long ears are needed to detect predators. In addition to their ears, rabbits have long, powerful hind legs and a short tail.

Rabbit fur is generally long and soft with colors ranging from shades of brown to gray.

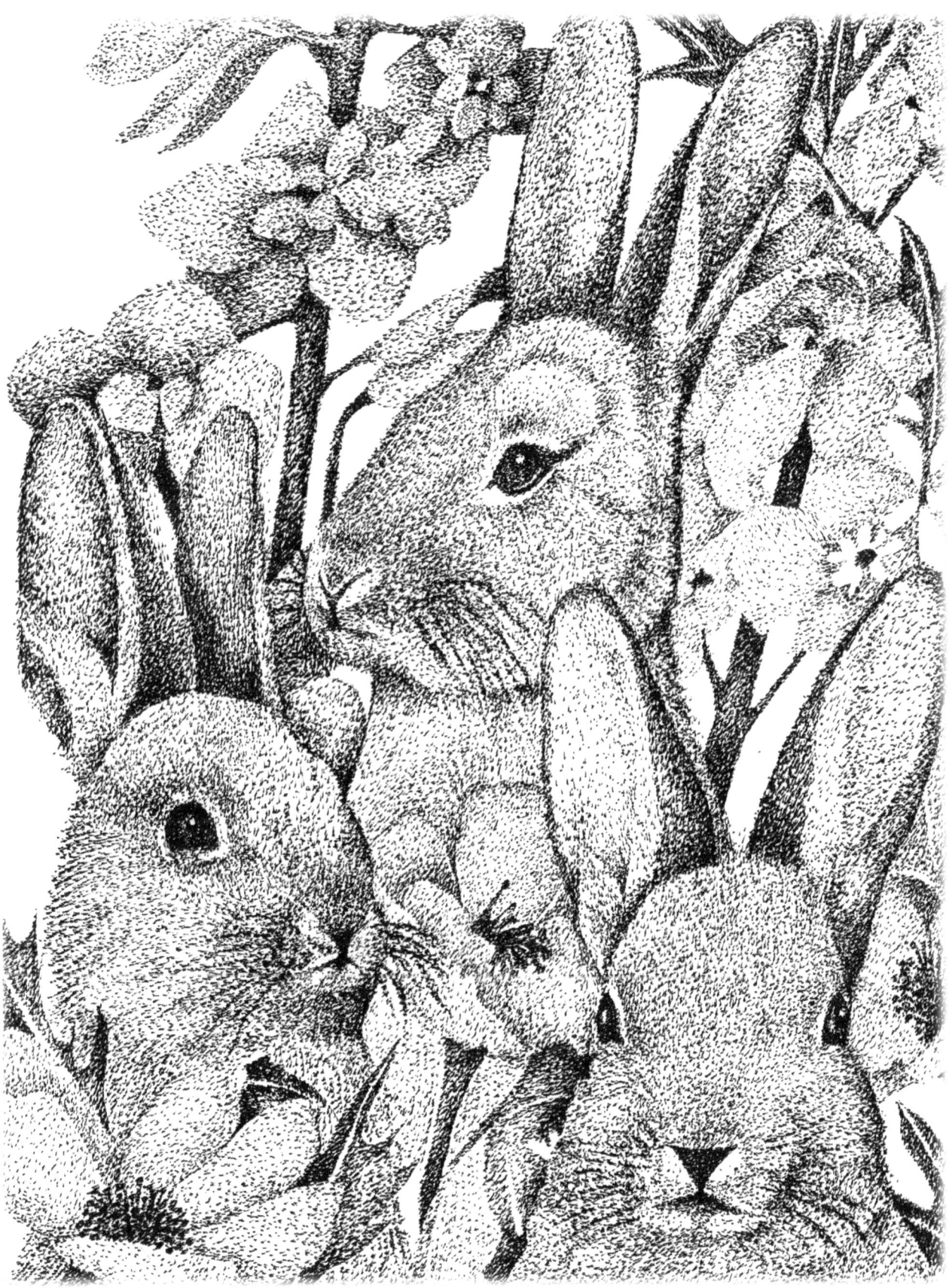

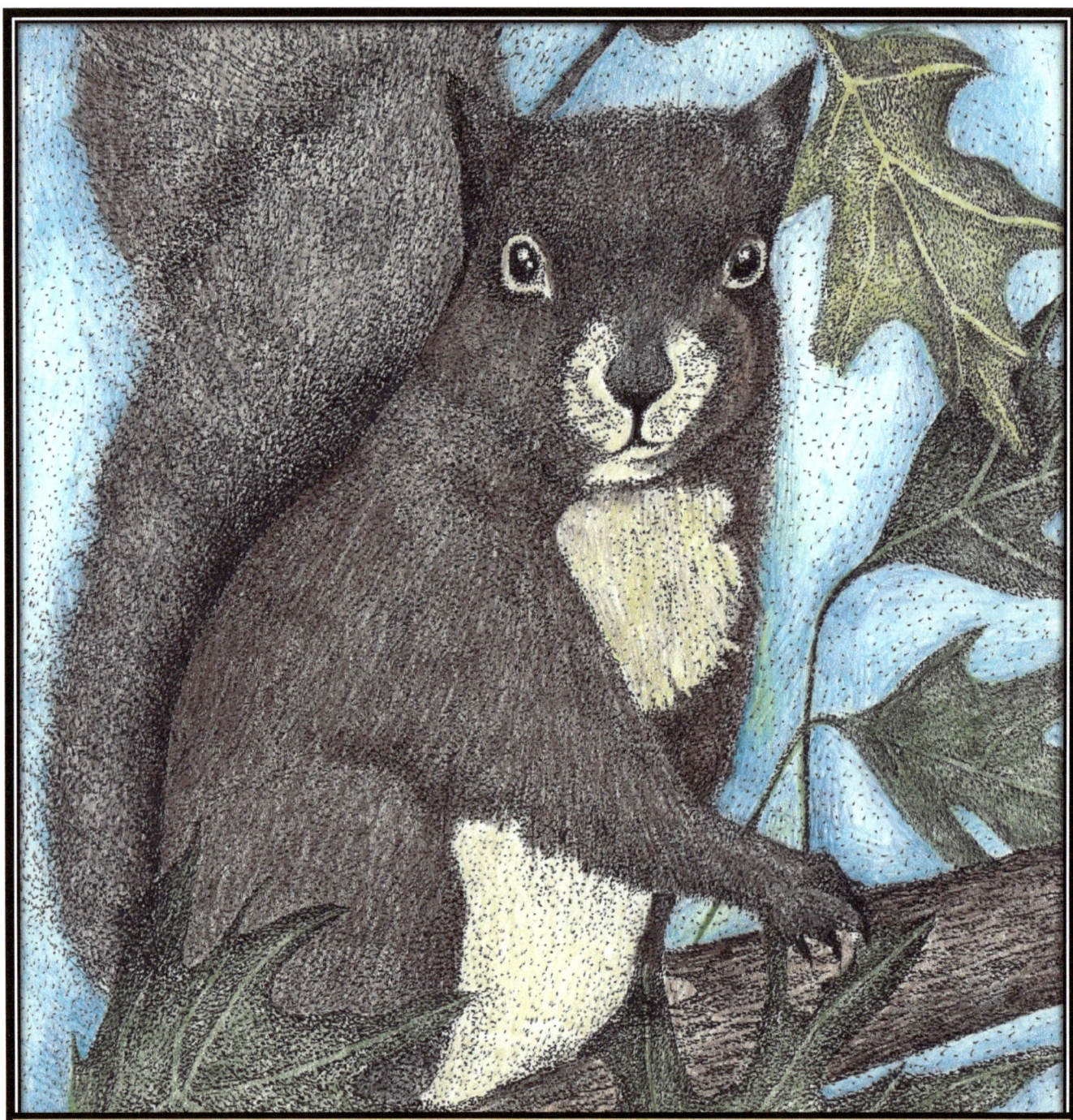

Squirrels

Every morning my dog Lola and I see numerous squirrels in the garden. They are always busy finding food and chasing each other through the trees. She loves to chase them, but never catches them as they are able to jump up to 20 feet and can run up to 20 miles per hour.

To prepare for the cold months, squirrels bury their food. Because they have prepared for the winter, they survive on their stored supplies. Squirrels like to eat both plants and meat. They mainly eat small insects, caterpillars, small animals and even young snakes.

Lola has no luck catching the squirrels, but she has chased a few up trees. Once they are sure they are out of her reach, they turn and squawk at her, as if they are scolding her for bothering them.

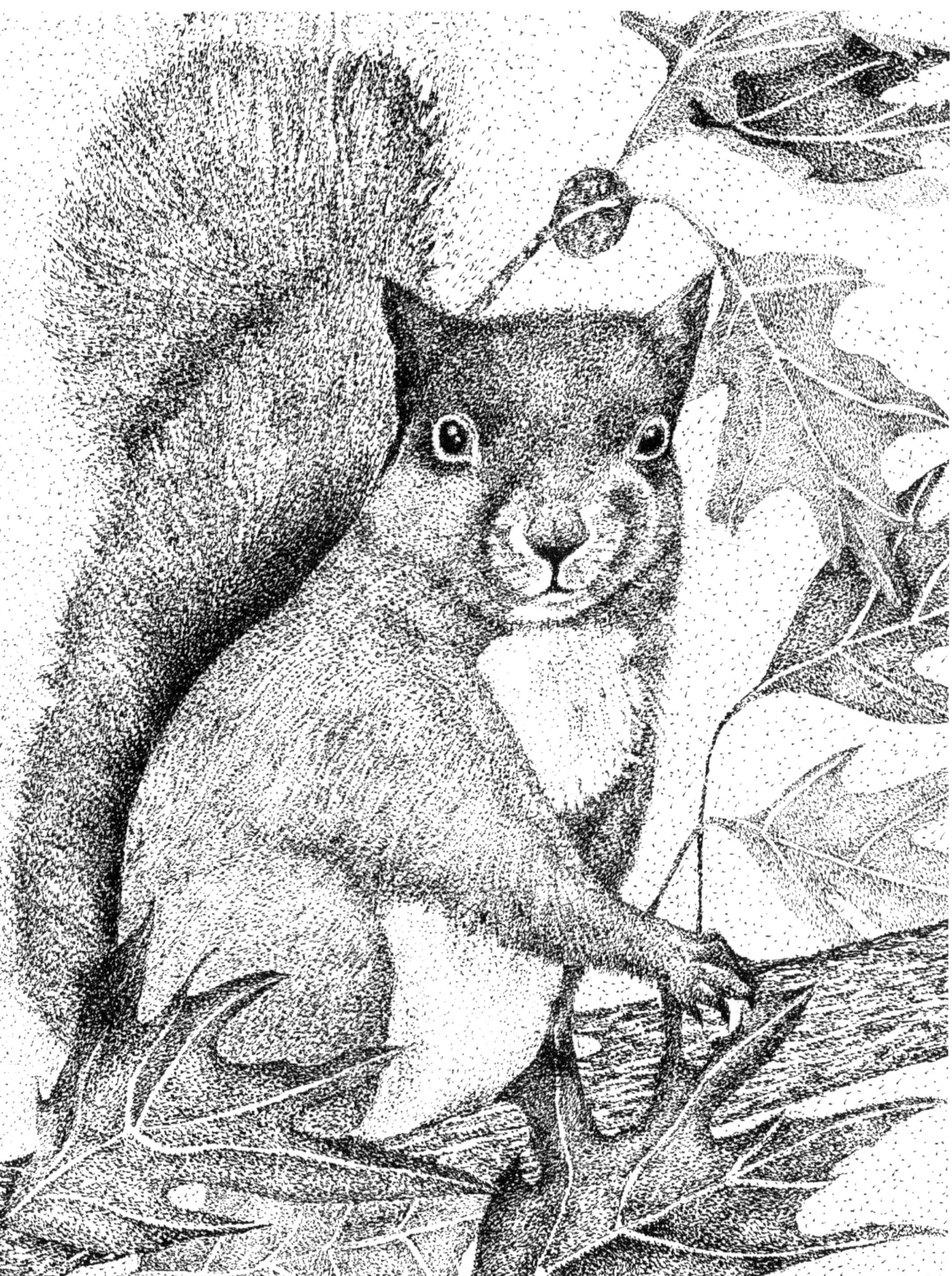

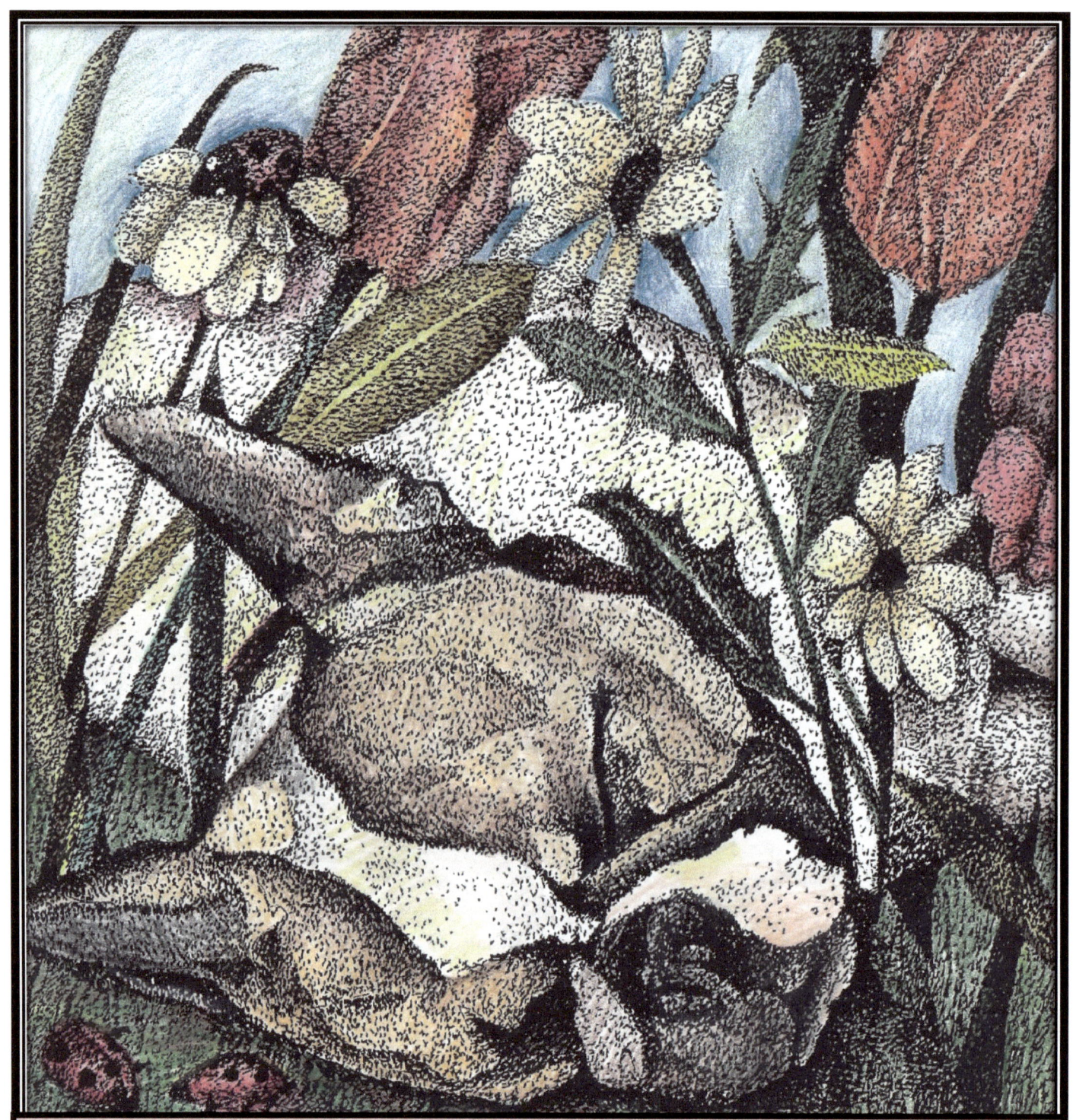

French Bulldog

This is Lola. I've drawn her sleeping in the garden, but she almost never does so. She is usually much too busy sniffing everything and chasing birds and squirrels!

French bulldogs were first bred in France in the late 1800's. They are a smaller version of the bulldog with large erect ears. French bulldogs are known for their affectionate nature, balanced disposition, and the ability to adapt to different surroundings.

Frenchies can overheat easily due to their short noses, so I am very careful about being outdoors in the Texas summer heat. That's fine with me. I don't like the heat either.

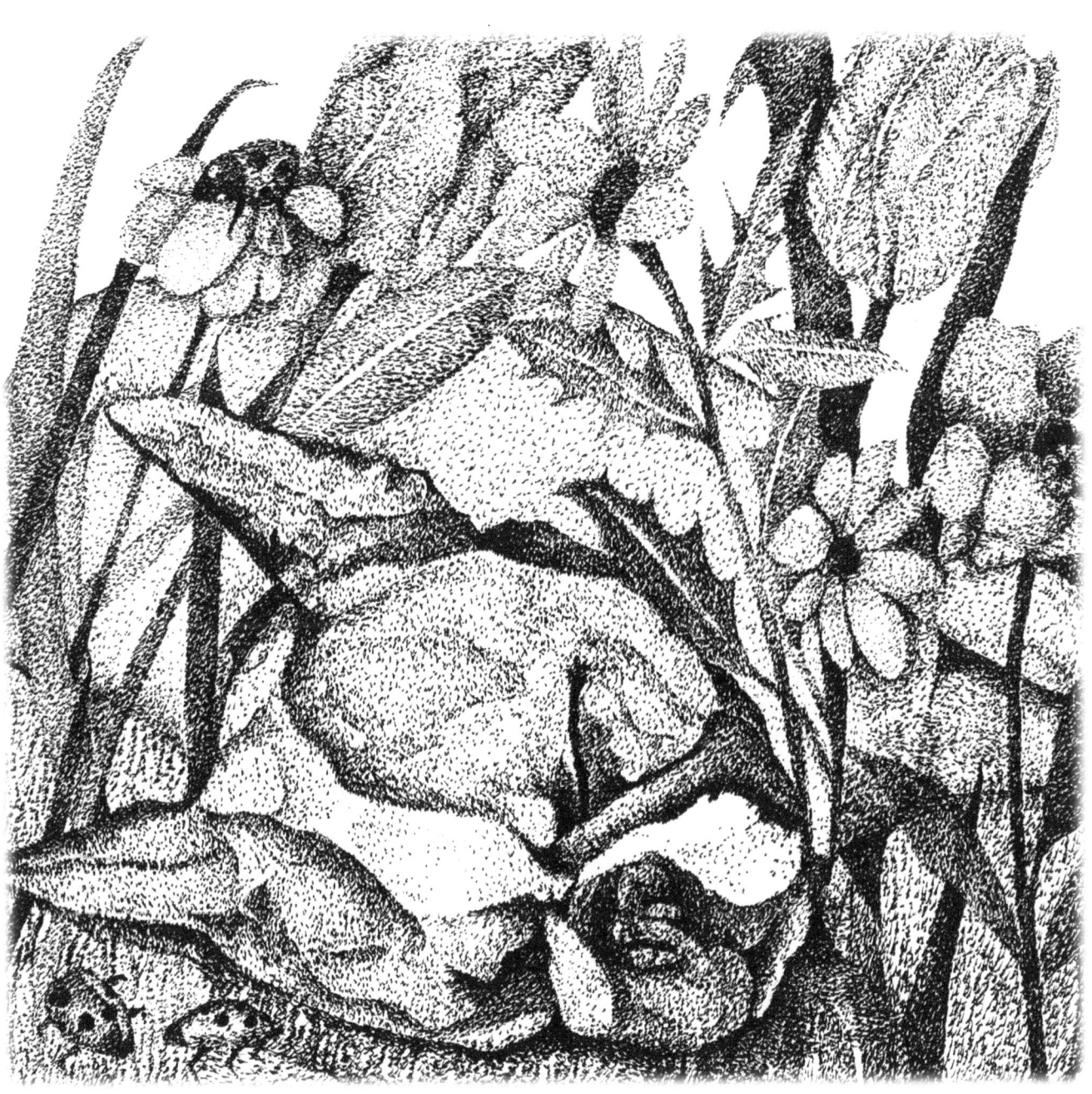

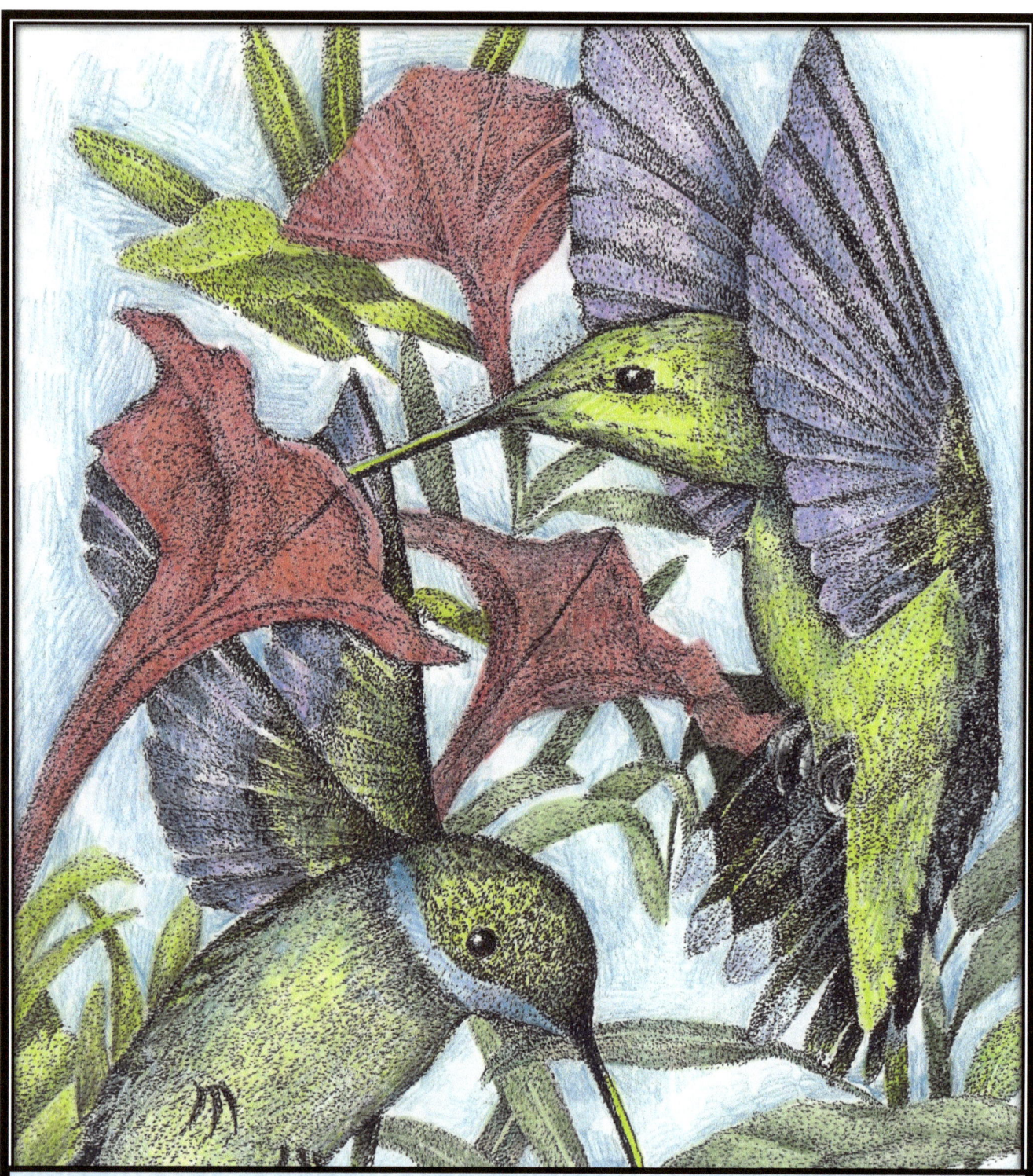

Hummingbirds

At first glance, it's easy to mistake a hummingbird for a large insect. They are some of the smallest birds in the world, yet they consume double their body weight every day. A hummingbird drinks nectar from hundreds of flowers and eats thousands of tiny insects daily.

It takes a lot of energy to flap their wings so rapidly. Hummingbirds can rotate their wings in a circle, allowing them to fly backwards, up, down, sideways and hover in midair. When not in flight, they often rest on branches and twigs.

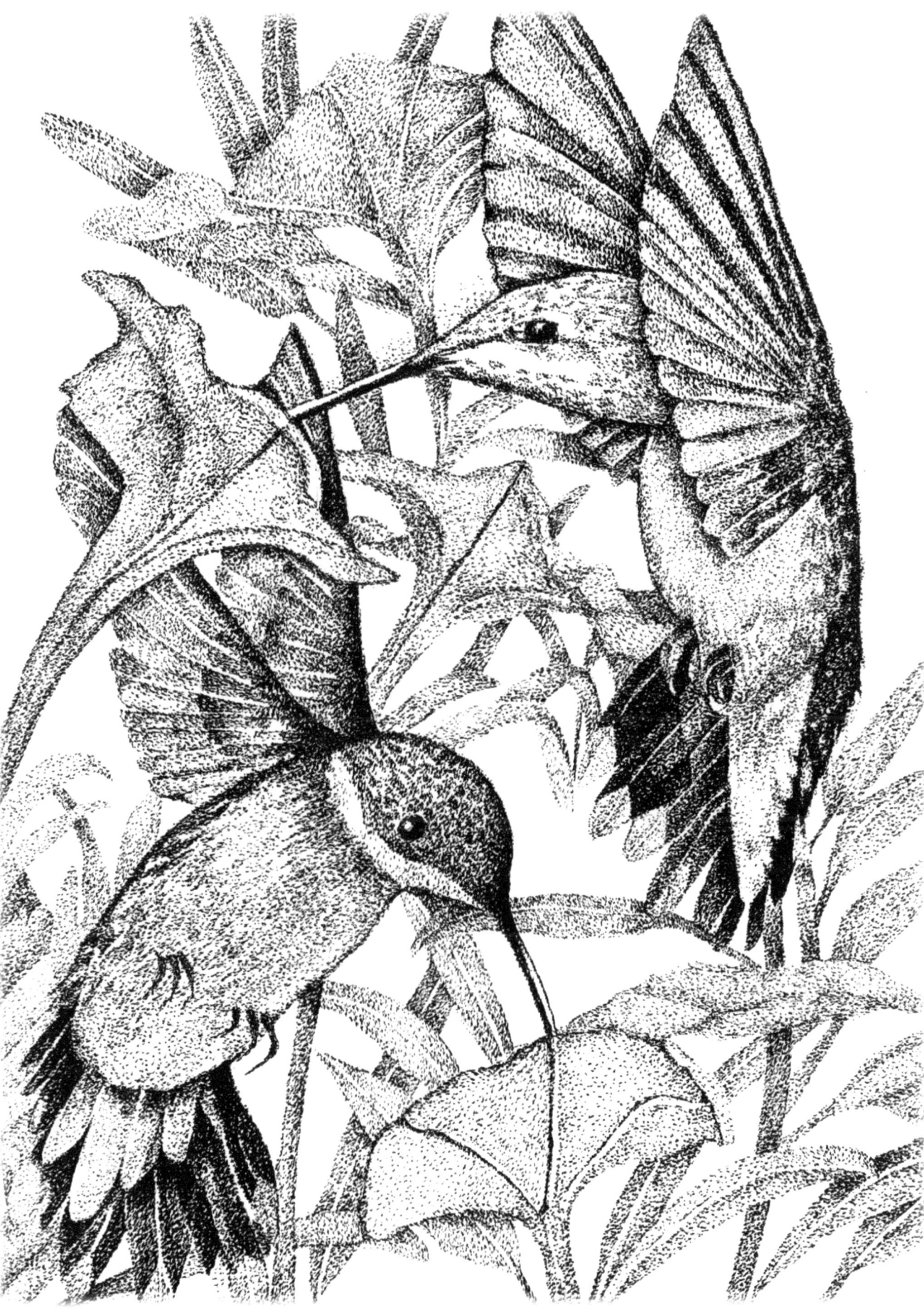

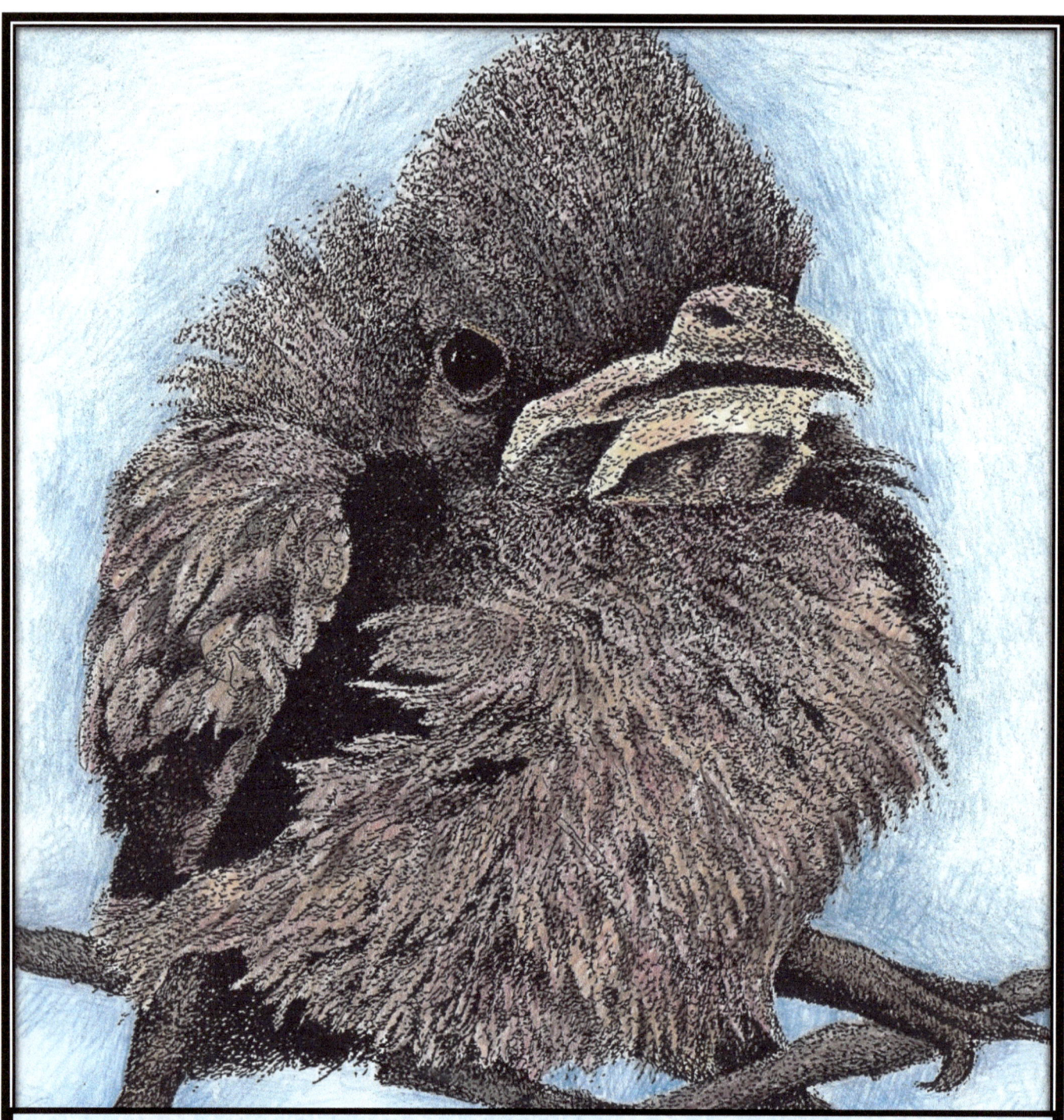

Baby Robin

Last summer, we found a baby robin on the ground who had fallen out of its nest. Although only 25% of robins live past their first year, this Robin was lucky. We put him in an open box and left him back where we found him. It wasn't long before his mother came and coaxed him to fly back to the nest.

Robins are one of the most common song birds. They are gray or brown with red breasts, with the males being more brightly colored than the females.

Robins eat berries, fruit, nuts, and seeds, but their favorite activity is snatching earthworms off the ground. They are present in most of North America, but prefer cooler climates. They migrate north every year because they do not like hot weather.

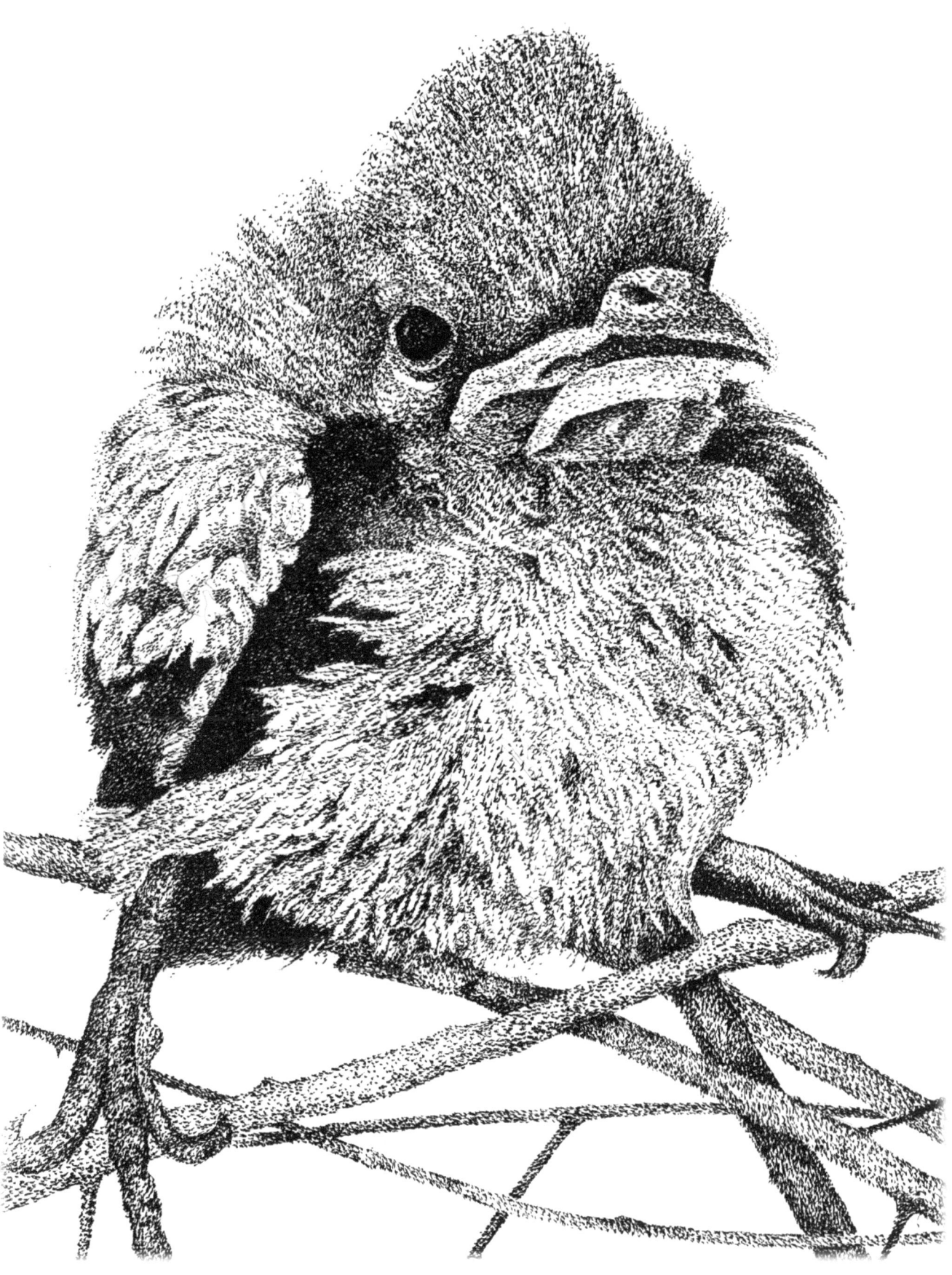

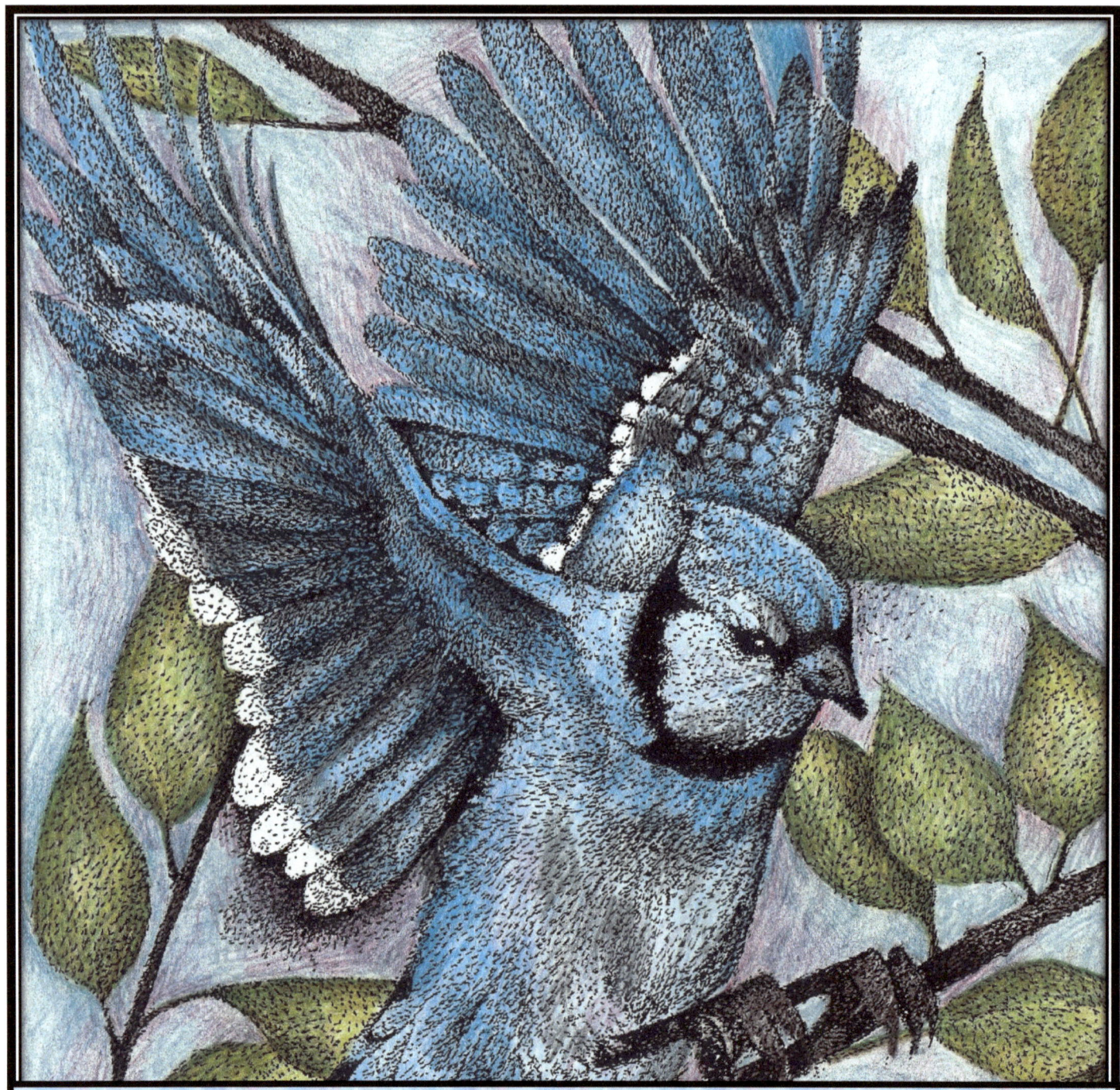

Blue Jay

Have you ever stepped outside and heard a loud bird call and maybe have seen a flash of bright blue in the sky. You may have seen or heard the beautiful blue jay. Males and females are the same striking color, while the males are a bit larger than the females. A pair of blue jays mate for life.

Blue jays are smart and are able to mimic the sound of the greatest predator, the hawk. They produce loud cries and screams than can sound like cats or even humans.

In Native American culture they are thought of as talkative, mysterious bird spirits. As animal spirit guides, the blue jay is said to encourage you to speak up and communicate what is on your mind.

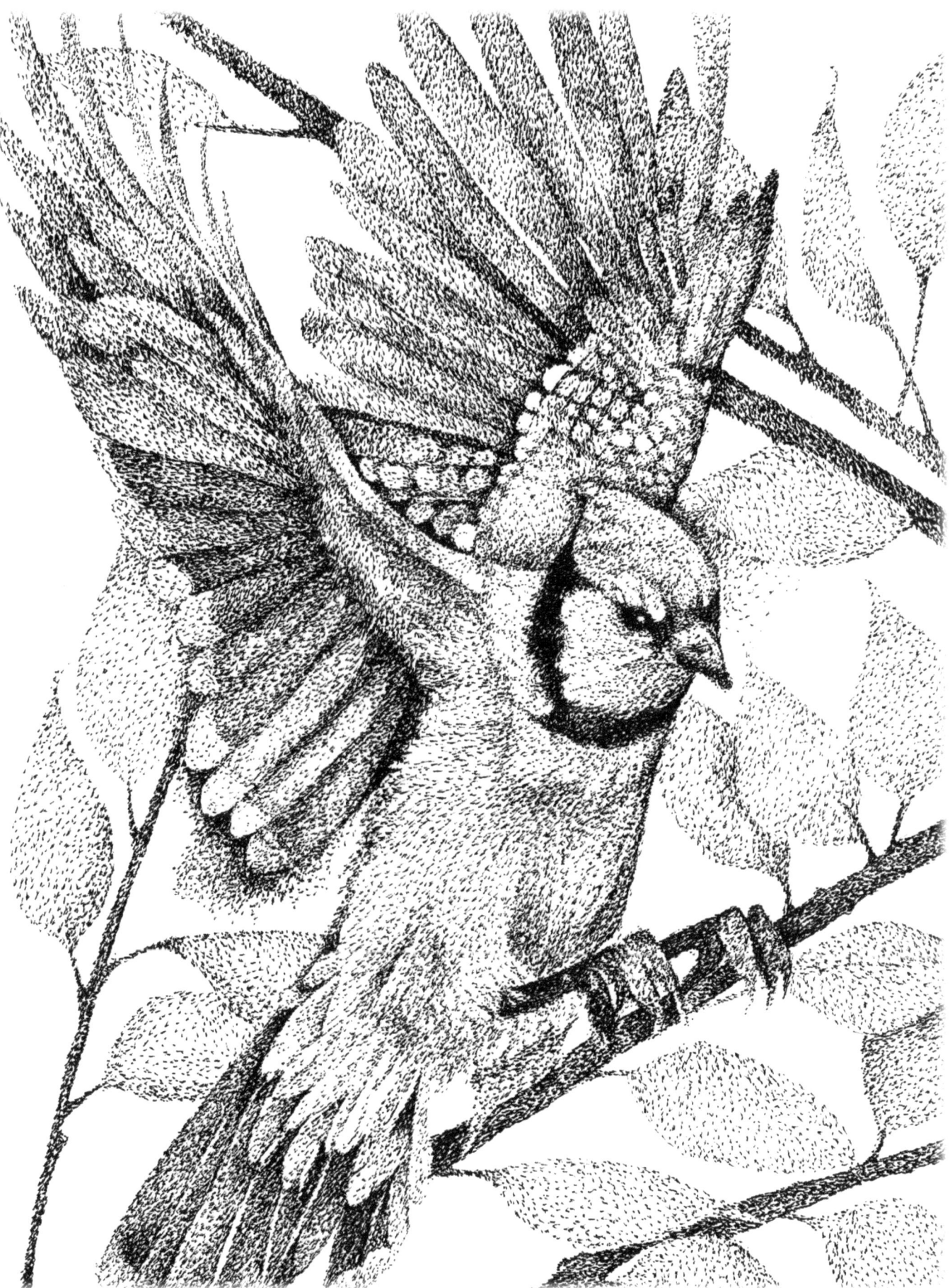

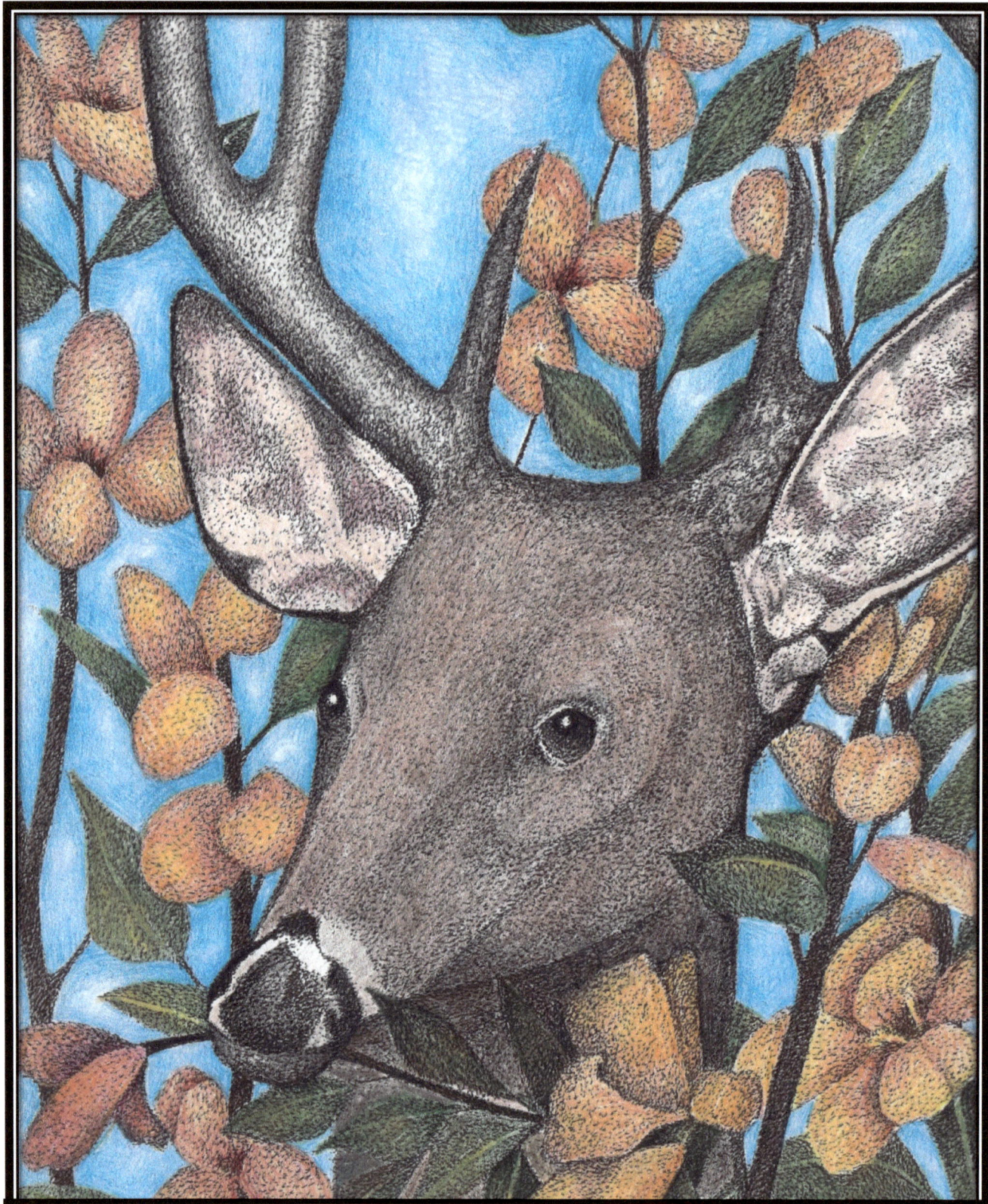

Deer

The deer is part of a group of hoofed animals that roam across most of the world. Deer are beautiful, graceful creatures with compact bodies with long, graceful legs and short tails. The males are called bucks or stags and, as adults, develop antlers. A female is called a hind or doe and, in some species of deer, can also have antlers.

Deer are highly selective plant eaters. They like high quality food, as many gardeners can confirm!

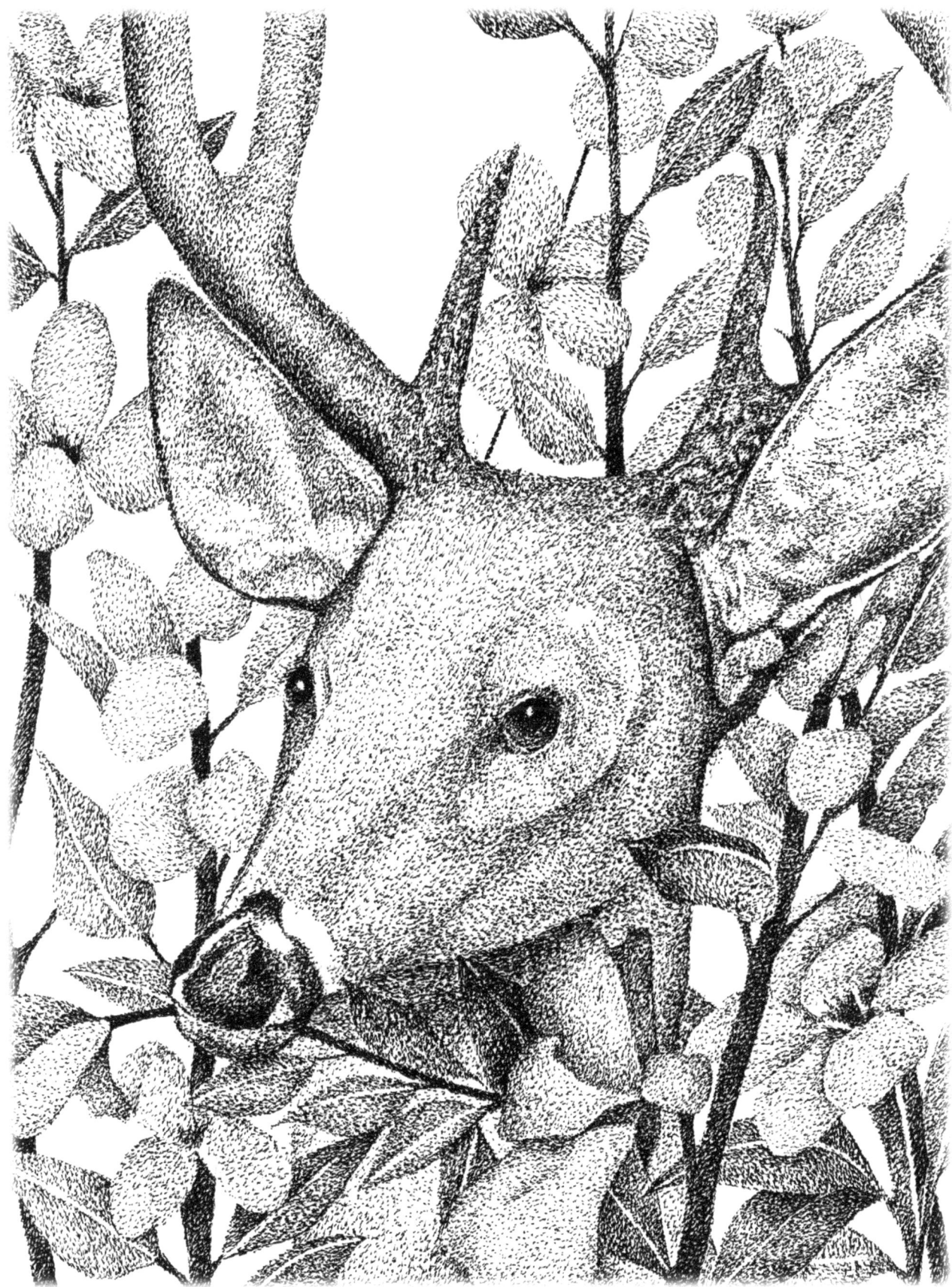

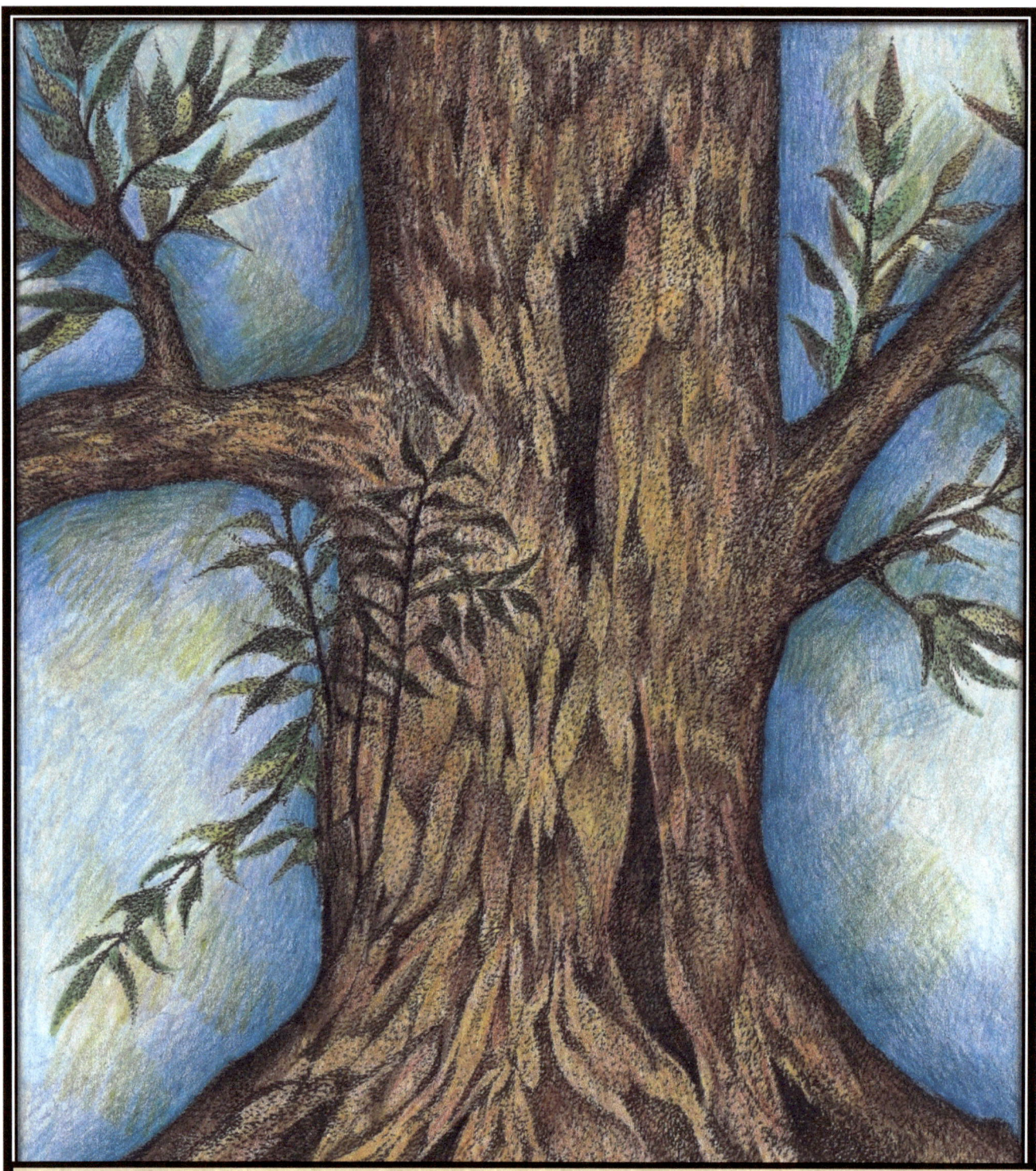

Trees

Human life could not exist if there were no trees. They are vital on earth. Trees bind the soil to prevent erosion. They break the force of the wind and rain while conserving rainwater. The shade they provide is said to be a calming influence on animals and humans. Trees provide habitats for many of earth's plants and creatures.

Most importantly, trees clean the air of pollutants and provide oxygen. They do all this, while adding immense beauty to our world.

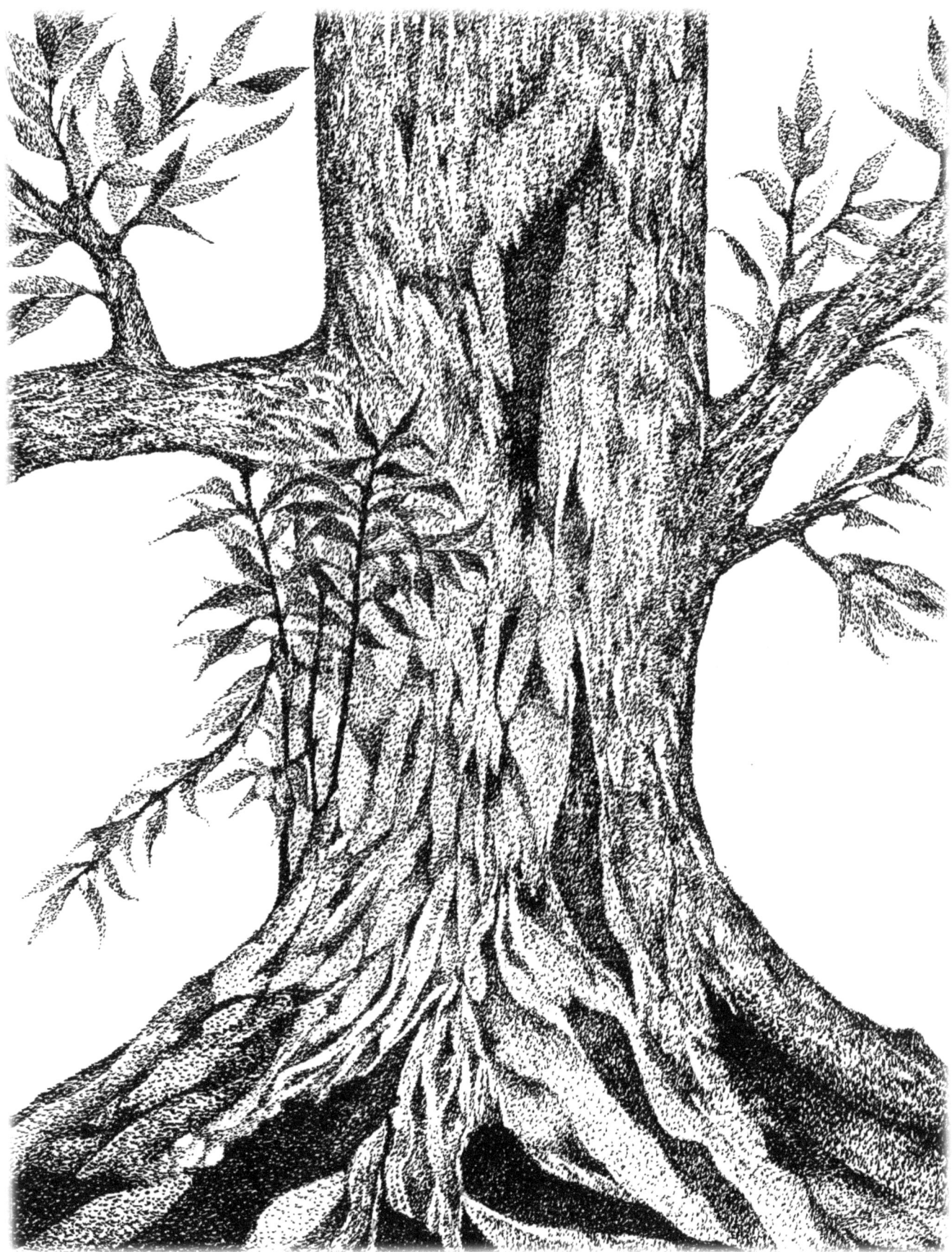

Jan Brieschke

Art teaching and the making of art in its many forms has been my passion since I was a small child. Art has sustained me, calmed me, and given me hope in many difficult situations as well as given me immense joy.

I grew up in the suburbs of Chicago and received my B.F.A. from Illinois Wesleyan University in Bloomington, Illinois. Later, I earned a Master's Degree in Art Education from the University of Houston.

I've taught in many schools and locations in my 28 years as an art teacher. In addition to public and private school teaching, I present workshops in watercolor, drawing, acrylics, colored pencil, and pen and ink.

In 2023 I published *Colors of Christmas: A Coloring Book for Adults and Teens* which provides a unique approach to a popular pastime using the stippling technique.

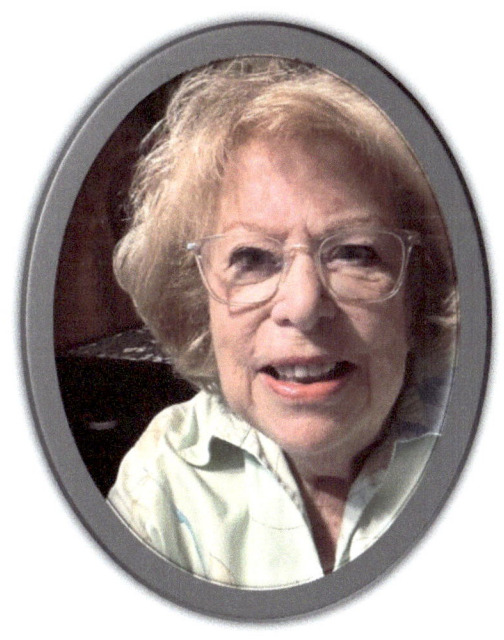